Teach Yourself With Open Learning

Teach Yourself With Open Learning

Derek Rowntree

KOGAN
PAGE

London • Philadelphia

First published in 1991 by Sphere.

This edition first published in 1993 by Kogan Page Ltd.

Kogan Page Limited
120 Pentonville Road
London N1 9JN

© Derek Rowntree, 1993

British Library Cataloguing in Publication Data

A CIP record for this book is available from the British Library.

ISBN 0 7494 1153 8

Typeset by the author
Printed and bound in Great Britain by
Clays Ltd, St Ives plc

Contents

Chapter 1

Welcome to open learning

Everybody seems to be doing open learning these days. But there's still a lot of confusion about just what is available and how to make best use of it. This book should help you sort it all out.

I'm glad you picked up this book. But I wonder why you did. I asked a few of the readers who used an earlier version. Here are some of the things they told me. Put a tick against any that sound at all like you:

☐ *"I've never done too well with other people trying to teach me; so the teach-yourself title was what got my interest."*

☐ *"I'm stuck at home with kids for the next year or two and, from what I've heard, open learning might be just what I should be getting into right now."*

☐ *"They say I could do some modules in my university course by open or distance learning; but what's that exactly? Would it suit the way I like to learn?"*

☐ *"There seems to be a mind-blowing amount of choice in open learning — I'm just hoping for guidance on what to do for the best."*

☐ *"I'm using a distance learning course to study for my promotion exams and I've got to the stage where I'm looking for any extra bit of help I can get ."*

☐ *"I've already done some computer-based training and my organization's setting up an open learning centre. So what might be in it for me?"*

☐ *"My boss has recommended me to do a supervisor's course by open learning so I thought I'd try to get an idea of what it would involve."*

What do you want from this book?

Clearly, open learning has a varied clientele. Do you have anything in common with any of those readers? Use the box below to make a note of your own reason for reading this book. What do you want from it?

```



```

In this book I am trying to speak to all users of open learning. I know there is something here for all the readers I've quoted above. If you are thinking of using open learning, you'll surely find that your concerns are dealt with also.

How to use this book

Of course you are free to use this book any way you please. I mean how could I stop you? But let me mention a few features you may find helpful:

Sequence I've written the book in such a way that there's no need for you to read the chapters in the order I've numbered them. My sequence seemed most logical to me, but it may not seem so to you. Feel free to dive in at whatever chapter most appeals to you. Nothing depends on your having read something else first — so you won't risk getting confused.

However much you get out of this book at first reading, you'll probably want to look at some sections again later on in your learning. Keep the book by you and use it whenever it seems helpful.

Previewing

No doubt you'll want to scan through the book — if you haven't already — to see the sort of material that lies ahead. You'll notice I've put in some big, bold headings every now and again. These are meant to help you plan your reading by seeing, at a glance, where each section within a chapter begins and ends.

"Activities"

You'll also notice that the book is not just for reading. You're expected to **write** in it as well. Every so often, you'll find empty boxes sticking out into the margin. I ask you to tick or write in these, so please keep a pencil handy while you read. We've had some boxes already. Did you make your mark in them?

Such invitations for you to do something are a vital part of open learning. They are usually called "activities". You may choose not to do some of them, of course. But the more you do, the more you may learn — because they should help you relate the ideas in the book to your own situation. And what you write may give you a useful record to look back on later.

Follow-up

You'll see that every chapter ends with what I've called "follow-up activities". These suggest some ways in which you might want to apply the ideas in each chapter.

Many of the follow-up activities suggest you make contact with other people. Open learning does not have to mean solitary learning. (See Chapter 8.)

Reflection

Also at the end of each chapter I have included a special "reflection" activity. Why have I done this? Because most people don't learn as much as they might from what they've studied — for the simple reason that they don't sit still for a minute or two afterwards and ask themselves what they've learned. Perhaps you suspect that you are not as reflective as you might be? If so, I hope a little practice will convince you of the benefits.

Objectives

You'll notice that every chapter after this one begins with a set of "objectives". These tell you what the chapter will help you learn to do. They're worth looking at before you read a chapter — to help you decide which bits of it you need. And also after you've read it — to check how much you've learned.

Like activities, objectives are also a very important feature of open learning materials.

I didn't list any objectives at the beginning of this chapter. But now you know what they are for, let me tell you the objectives for this book as a whole:

The objectives of this book

This book should enable you to:

☐ Be clear about what and why you want to learn.

☐ Say what open learning is and what benefits it might offer you.

☐ Be realistic about the demands this type of learning may make on you.

☐ Decide whether you would like to do some open learning.

☐ List your own preferences and needs from an open learning programme.

☐ Track down open learning packages that suit your needs and preferences.

☐ Deal confidently with open learning providers.

☐ Judge how well the support services offered by a provider might fit your needs.

☐ Choose an appropriate open learning programme (package plus support services).

☐ Use appropriate strategies in tackling your open learning package.

☐ Make best use of people who can support you in your open learning.

☐ Evaluate the programme while you are learning from it and when you have completed it.

☐ Reflect on your open learning experience and decide how to build upon it.

Tick off any of the above objectives that seem to tie in with your interest in this book. Is there anything else you want to be able to do as a result of reading this book? If so, make a note of it in the box:

If you want to be able to do things that aren't on the list of objectives, I hope the book will help you with them anyway. If not, I think it may help you see other ways of learning how — perhaps by discussing your needs with other people.

Getting into open learning

Open learning seems to be cropping up everywhere these days. I don't know if you saw the first *Superman* film. If you did, you may have noticed how our infant hero was kept gainfully occupied throughout his intergalactic journey from Krypton to Smallsville, USA — with a distance learning package.

And, in the real world, open learning is booming. In Britain alone, there could easily be a million learners at any one time studying largely by themselves with self-teaching packages made up of texts, audio and video materials, and sometimes computers. Some are learning at home, some in college or university, some at work.

The Open University, which began in 1971, has something approaching 200,000 students at present. Its continuing success has led many other universities to offer some of their courses by open or distance learning. Other national organizations like the Open College, National Extension College and Open College of the Arts each serves thousands of learners every year.

And there are yet more: hundreds of local colleges and other providers are enrolling open learners all over Britain. Schools are using open learning materials for teaching 16-19 year olds. And many large employers — e.g. B & Q, the NHS, British Gas, W.H. Smith, Rover cars, ICI, the Post Office, and many high street banks and building societies — now use open learning as a regular part of their training.

You can study almost anything by open learning — from accountancy to Arabic; from computer science to zoo management; from sculpture to marine biology. In fact, the day may soon be here when you can't study anything **without** doing some open learning. Perhaps all courses will include some.

Many people are doing open learning without even knowing it. It doesn't always go by that name. Here are some of the commoner names. Tick any that you have already been involved in — or may be involved in soon:

- [ ] Distance learning
- [ ] Flexi-study
- [ ] Flexible learning
- [ ] Self-instruction
- [ ] Supported self-study
- [ ] Packaged courses
- [ ] Learning by appointment
- [ ] Resource-based learning
- [ ] Computer-based training
- [ ] Correspondence courses
- [ ] Open learning

Open learning and distance learning are probably the two most common names. But schemes going by any of the other names in the list will also operate in much the same way. So may a scheme with a totally different name altogether.

So what do they all have in common? Just the fact that you'll be doing most of your learning from **packages** — from expertly designed teaching materials — rather than from a live teacher. In a distance learning scheme, for example, you may rarely meet a teacher at all. Flexible learning, on the other hand, may mix work on packages with "ordinary" class-work.

As an open learner you'll be expected to **teach yourself** — with a lot of help from a package and varying amounts of help from other people.

Not everyone who tries it will warm to that idea. But most do. The rest of this book should help you decide whether you will be one of them.

Reflection box

Here's where I ask you to look back over the chapter and reflect for a minute or two. What do you feel is the most useful thing you've got from this chapter? How might you apply it? Make a note in the box:

Follow-up activities

1. Look out for mentions of open learning (by any of its names) in the press and elsewhere. Now that you've started thinking about it, you'll probably see references all over the place.

2. Talk about open learning to your friends and workmates. You may find some of them will admit to having been at it for some time. What can they tell you about it?

3. Read the other chapters in this book!

Chapter 2

You and your learning

We're all of us learning every day of our lives. But not everyone goes in for organized learning. What might you want from it? What will it cost you? And how can you use your experience of everyday learning to succeed as an open learner?

Objectives:

When you've worked through this chapter you should be better able to:

- Identify the benefits you expect to get from learning.
- Recognize the costs involved.
- Evaluate other ways of achieving your goals.
- Identify the learning skills you use every day that will be needed in your open learning programme.

We can't not learn!

No really, we don't have any choice about learning. We are learning every day of our lives — usually without even thinking about it. We gain new knowledge from reading newspapers and watching television and chatting with friends. We develop skills in hobbies and sports. Our attitudes to certain people change as we learn more about them. And, if we have jobs, we become better and better at them.

But all this is casual learning. It's rather different from an organized, systematic course of study. With such a course — or "programme" as we'll call it in this book — your chief purpose is to learn:

- You'll start off knowing you want or need to learn something.

- You'll have a good idea of what kind of knowledge or skills you are trying to attain.

- You'll expect to undertake various activities that help you learn them.

- And you'll have ways of checking whether or not you have succeeded in learning.

Why do you want to learn?

So, I'll assume you've either started on a systematic learning programme or are thinking of doing so. What do you hope to get out of it? Write down your aim(s) or reason(s) in the box below:

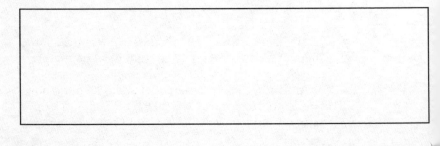

There are many reasons for deciding to start on a systematic learning programme. It's worth giving some thought to just what yours are. This will help you to choose a suitable programme. And, even if you don't have much choice, it will help you decide how best to tackle the programme. For instance, you may be able to skip bits that don't meet your needs.

Here is a list of reasons for learning which I've put together from the comments of several open learners. Tick those that would also be true of you:

☐ A. I need a qualification.
☐ B. I hope to get a better job.
☐ C. I hope to perform better in my present job.
☐ D. I hope to get a job.
☐ E. I've always liked to study.
☐ F. I'm very keen on my subject.
☐ G. I want to widen my horizons.
☐ H. I want to make up for what I missed earlier in life.
☐ I. I want to meet new people.
☐ J. I need a new challenge in life.
☐ K. I want to prepare for community service.
☐ L. I want to prove that I've got what it takes.
☐ M. My boss told me I should be doing it.
☐ N. I did poorly at this when I was younger; but I think I'll crack it this time.
☐ O. I want somebody to tell me that I'm as smart as I think I am.
☐ P. I want to take my mind off domestic and work worries.

Clearly, there are many good reasons for starting on a programme of learning. Apart from what you wrote yourself, you may have ticked several items in the list above. For instance, I recently set about learning how to do word-processing. My chief reason was to help me do my work better (item C). But I also wanted to

prove to myself that I could master the computer
(item L). And I soon found that learning about word-
processing put me in touch with a wide network of
people I would not otherwise have met (item I).

The more reasons you've got for learning, the better.
If the going gets tough and you're only learning
because your boss says you should, you might find it
difficult to put in the necessary energy. Fortunately,
whatever reasons you may have for starting on a
learning programme, you'll often find that unexpected
benefits pop up once you are under way. Even a
course you start on to please the boss can turn out to
be a lot of fun and very useful to you.

What will it cost you?

They say there's no gain without pain. And every
organized learning programme has its costs — time,
money, energy, and so on. Even if your employer
offers you a "free" training programme, it will still
cost you one way or another.

I don't want to put you off organized learning. It may
be just what you need. And, in the long run, the costs
of not doing it — the lost opportunities — may be
greater than the costs of doing it.

But it would be unwise to leap in without thinking
about the likely costs and how you will meet them. For
instance, if you've already got a programme in mind,
which of the following possible costs might you have
to meet?

- [ ] A. Course fees.
- [ ] B. Cost of books, equipment, etc.
- [ ] C. Examination or accreditation fees.
- [ ] D. Travelling costs.
- [ ] E. Overnight accommodation costs.
- [ ] F. Payments to child-minders, etc.

☐ G. Loss of pay due to time off work.
☐ H. Your time. (How many hours per week, for how many weeks?)
☐ I. Your energy and commitment. (Will it leave you enough for other purposes?)
☐ J. The goodwill of your partner, family, friends and colleagues.

Others (What?):

Cash!

For some learners, the financial costs (A-G) will be the big concern. Such costs will obviously vary a great deal — from the cost of attending the local FE college one evening a week to the much greater cost of a full-time three year degree course at university. (Subject for subject, open learning programmes usually cost less than "ordinary" courses.) Some learners may need to allow for a temporary but noticeable drop in their standard of living.

However, some financial support **may** be available from employers, local education authorities, the Employment Department, and others. (More about this in Chapter 5 — see page 91.)

Time & Energy

For other learners, time, energy and commitment (H and I) may seem the major cost area. Where can they find the necessary hours? Can they summon up the necessary motivation? We all have only 24 hours in a day and we mostly think our energy and commitment are also limited. What we spend in one area we can't spend in another. Do we really desire the goals of the learning programme enough to redirect our energies?

Actually, once learners get involved in a programme that fires their enthusiasm they often find that their energy budget is not limited after all. They manage to create extra energy — not just for the learning programme but for other things in their lives as well. But you can't rely on this happening. For many learners, even a very rewarding programme turns out to be a hard slog — especially if their work and families continue to make heavy demands.

Nearest & dearest

Finally, for many learners, the costs most difficult to bear are not to do with either money or time and energy. They are to do with the emotional hassle of balancing the demands of their learning programme against the demands of their near ones and dear ones. As an adult learner, you may get a great deal of support and encouragement from your partner, family, friends and colleagues. But, on the other hand, they may give you resentment and hassle because you are not so available to satisfy their needs as you used to be. They may also pooh-pooh the whole idea of what you are doing — you're getting above yourself or you're wasting your time.

It's easy to feel guilty about letting other people down. You can start wondering whether it really is worthwhile — or just a selfish dream you are pursuing. This can be a particular problem if you are a woman, of course — because social pressures may have conditioned you to believe your prime duty is to serve the needs of others. You may need to be pretty assertive and have a strong sense of your goals if you are to spend the necessary time and energy on your own needs — especially if you are only too aware that it's your partner's earnings that are financing your learning. (But could your partner earn so much if you weren't providing back-up at home?)

How else might you get what you want?

Organized learning may be exactly what you need to achieve your goals in life. But it seems only fair to remind you that there may be other ways of getting what you are looking for. Some of these ways may be quicker, less costly or more agreeable than taking on a course of study. Or maybe you'll want to do them **as well** as a learning programme.

For instance, think through the possibilities in the following list. Tick any that might help you get the sorts of benefit you'd hope to get from an organized learning programme:

☐ Try to get my present job changed (e.g. more responsibility).

☐ Move to a different job in my organization.

☐ Move to a job in a different organization.

☐ Get a job.

☐ Set aside more time for pursuing my own interests (e.g. local history or computers).

☐ Join a club concerned with my special interest.

☐ Make more systematic use of the resources in my public library.

☐ Travel more, both in the UK and abroad.

☐ Take up a new sport or outdoor activity, e.g. sailing or hill-walking.

☐ Change my diet or my health habits.

☐ Volunteer for work in the community, e.g. Mencap or Victim Support.

☐ Setting myself a challenge that does not depend on book learning.

And if that list gives you further ideas that I haven't suggested, jot them down in the box overleaf:

What I'm getting at here is that there may be other ways to achieve some of your purposes than to undertake a formal learning programme. Not all of them will obtain all the benefits you might seek, of course. For instance, joining a club is unlikely to lead to a qualification. Working in the community or travelling more may not help you improve in your present job — though it's possible that they might. On the other hand, such alternatives might well give you all you want in the way of wider horizons, new challenges and meeting people.

One last point: many of the alternatives I've listed— new jobs or sports, and community work, for example — can themselves require you to undertake an organized programme of training. And all will involve you in some kind of learning.

Build on your learning skills

Before you start on a systematic programme of learning, it's worth asking yourself what experience you bring with you to the project. Why? Because you can build on that experience in your new learning.

You may have done a lot of organized learning in recent years—and with some success. Or you may have done very little. You may have done a lot some years ago but now feel your skills may have got rusty. You may never have done very much — and what you did do you perhaps did under protest and with less satisfaction than you might have liked.

People who haven't done much studying will often lack confidence. They may feel they won't be good at learning because they weren't good at it in the past or because they don't have any qualifications. But they are wrong. They simply don't notice how good they are at learning — informal, everyday learning.

Everyday learning

If you have done some systematic learning lately you may well feel you've got experience that you can draw on in an open learning programme. But what if you don't have any recent experience? And what if your last experience of formal learning was not a total success? Well, I would guess that you still have some recent experience of successful learning — in your home life, in sports and hobbies, in your work:

- Maybe you've learned to do a new job.
- Maybe you've had to learn the ways of a new spare-time activity you've taken up.
- Maybe you've learned to cook certain dishes or to drive a car (or even programme a video-recorder).

Think of something you've learned in the last year. This can be something you've learned on a course or something you've taught yourself informally. Think back over your experience, using the following questions to guide you:

- What prompted you to learn it?
- How did you set about learning it?
- What people or resources did you get help from?
- What kind of help did you get?
- What kind of difficulties or problems did you meet?
- How did you handle any difficulties or problems?
- How did you judge how effectively you were learning?
- How did you feel about your ability to learn?

So what does that learning experience tell you about yourself? List some of the skills and approaches you have that might help you in a systematic learning programme — e.g. the skills of planning your time or of making sense of instruction manuals.

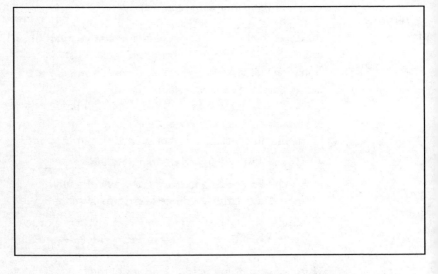

I hope you found plenty to write — because you've probably got more skills than you might have imagined. For instance, which of the following can you do — usually, sometimes or never?:

I believe I can:

	Usually	Sometimes	Never
• decide what I want	☐	☐	☐
• plan how to get it	☐	☐	☐
• set a timetable for myself	☐	☐	☐
• alter my plans if circumstances change	☐	☐	☐
• persuade other people to help me	☐	☐	☐
• listen to other people's ideas	☐	☐	☐
• learn from critics of my work	☐	☐	☐
• concentrate on what interests me	☐	☐	☐
• get hooked on solving a problem	☐	☐	☐

- persevere when I run into difficulties
- be realistic about how I am getting on
- work on my own
- get information from books and magazines and/or television
- remember things that interest me
- follow technical instructions
- write letters or reports
- apply what I have learned to my work

How did you get on with that list of skills? (Perhaps you wouldn't have thought of some of them as being learning skills at all.) Did it contain many that weren't on your own list? If so, were you able to say "Usually" or "Sometimes" to quite a few of them?

**D-I-Y
learning**

The fact is, the skills mentioned in that list are just the sort you'll need on an open learning programme. Most of them are to do with being self-reliant. With open learning (even if you're doing it at college or university) there'll be no one breathing down your neck to get you to learn. Whether or not you learn depends on you. That's why you're off to a good start if you are already in the habit of teaching yourself.

If you're not, you'll soon learn how to. An open learning programme is put together in such a way as to help you organize your own learning and become your own teacher. Even by the time you've finished this book, you'll probably be able to rub out some of the ticks you may have put in the "Never" column!

Chapter 3 of this book tells you what an open learning programme can offer you that "ordinary" courses cannot. And Chapter 4 tells you how open learning helps you to learn. As you'll see, there is nothing weird or mysterious about it. Open learning builds on the learning you've been doing all your life.

Reflection box

Look back at the objectives at the beginning of this chapter. Do you feel reasonably confident about them? What is the most useful thing you've got from this chapter? How might you apply it?

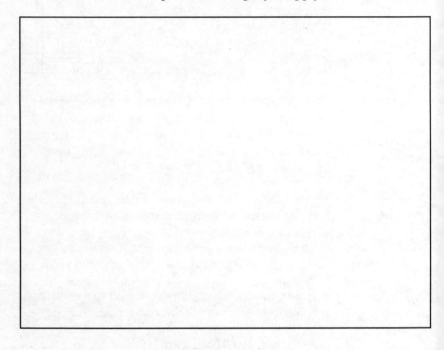

Follow-up activities

1. Start thinking, if you haven't already, about:
   - why you want to learn;
   - what you want to learn; and
   - how much time and money you can devote to learning over the next few weeks/months.
2. Next time you learn something in everyday life, reflect on the experience and ask yourself what skills you used in that learning.

Chapter 3

What can open learning offer you?

Open learning programmes are different from "ordinary" courses. What's special about them? And what do they offer you that ordinary courses can't?

Objectives:

When you've worked through this chapter you should be able to:

- Say what the main idea is behind open learning.

- Assess how open is the learning programme you are on at present (if you are on one) or any programme you may be about to start.

- Suggest ways in which you would like a future learning programme to be open — or how you would like your present programme to be made more open.

- Decide what features you will look for in an open learning programme.

What is open learning?

"Open learning" is a new slogan used by certain teachers and trainers. They use it to suggest the intention behind the kind of learning schemes they are offering. What they are trying to open up is new OPPORTUNITIES for learning. There are two parts to this:

1. People who are already used to learning will get more opportunities to learn.

2. People who have not previously thought of themselves as learners will get new opportunities.

How do teachers and trainers try to open up these new learning opportunities? They do it by removing or lowering certain **barriers** that prevent people learning from "ordinary" courses. What sort of barriers, you may ask?

Think of something you were once quite keen to learn but didn't — e.g. how to play the guitar, speak a foreign language, train for a promotion. Maybe you started on a course but didn't complete it. Perhaps you gave up the idea before you even started. Can you think of one or more barriers that prevented you from learning?

See if the barriers you mentioned are among those listed opposite:

Ten common barriers to learning

"Ordinary" education and training put up many barriers that prevent some people from learning. Tick any of the following that you have suffered from:

☐ **Lack of information**

You may have been unable to find out even that a suitable course existed, let alone what it might offer you or what it would demand of you. And if you did get to hear about it, how could you be sure it was for you? You may not have been able to sample it — e.g. by attending a typical class or trying some of the set work. If you didn't know anyone else who'd been on the course and could tell you about it, you may have been unwilling to commit yourself.

☐ **Unsuitable content**

Perhaps the course coverage was not quite to your liking. Maybe it covered tourist's French when you wanted business French, or folk guitar when you wanted to learn ragtime. Maybe it covered too much, or too little, or was at not quite the right level for you. Few courses can adapt themselves to the needs of individual learners.

☐ **Unsuitable methods**

Maybe the course depended too much on teaching methods you don't care for — e.g. lecturing, discussion groups, books, practical work. For various reasons, we all have our preferred ways of learning and we may be turned off by courses that don't use them.

☐ **The qualifications gap**

Maybe the course looked all right for you but you were deemed unsuitable for the course. Many ordinary courses are open only to people who have successfully taken certain previous courses. For example, many degree courses demand certain A level grades as an entrance requirement.

☐ **Timing**

Maybe the course wasn't available just when you wanted it. That is, you may have had to delay your start or else start before you really wanted to. And maybe it was only available at times you couldn't manage — e.g. during working hours or at weekends when the family has first call on your time. Perhaps also the course met too frequently to suit your personal timetable. Or maybe you started the course and found it was going too fast for you, or too slowly.

☐ **Place**

Maybe you ruled out the course because of the travelling you had to do to get to it. Ordinary courses aren't held in our own homes, so they usually require us to make a journey. Have you ever struggled across town in the depths of winter to attend some college or training centre — or even braved the freezing fog to come in from some outlying village? It can make you wonder whether the learning you're getting is really worth the trouble. Sometimes the only suitable course isn't even in the same town. You might have to travel to the other end of the country or even go abroad.

☐ **Costs**

Apart from the travelling costs, you also have to consider the course fee, the cost of any books or equipment you need and, sometimes, the cost of time off work or of lost overtime. This may well have been enough to put you off some courses — especially if some of the other barriers were also bugging you.

☐ **Anxiety**

Most adults feel some anxiety at the thought of taking up learning again after what may be a long lay off. And their memories of the last time they experienced learning (e.g. in school) may not be very happy ones. They may remember embarrassment, humiliation and a sense of failure. If so, they won't fancy signing up for more courses and perhaps being made to look stupid all over again.

Even if you were successful in your earlier education
you may wonder if you've still got the capacity for it.
You may be reluctant to sit in a class alongside
younger people who have more recent practice at that
sort of learning. If those younger people are your
workmates, you may be even more wary. And, of
course, you may or may not feel ready for all the new
social relationships with other members of a class that
conventional courses are likely to get you into.

Domestic pressures
You may have given up on an ordinary course because
of family or friends. If you have children or other
adults to look after, getting to courses that meet in the
evening or at weekends can be a big problem. Getting
to courses that demand full-time attendance away
from home can be quite impossible for many people. If
your family and friends resent your spending time
away from them, your motivation to go on a course
can be heavily undermined.

Physical disabilities
If you have a physical disability you may find that
many ordinary courses are difficult for you to attend.
If a person has problems with seeing and hearing, then
reading books and listening to lectures are out. For
anyone in a wheelchair, what are the chances of
getting it into a classroom? Travelling to the college
or training centre may be quite impossible anyway.

You may have thought of yet other barriers that aren't
listed above. There certainly are plenty of them
around. Each one makes it a little more likely that
someone, somewhere will feel unable to join an
ordinary course or unable to stick with it once they
have joined.

No single open learning programme will reduce all
these barriers. But the more it lowers them, the more
open it is. The more people will be able to benefit from
that programme.

How open learning breaks the barriers

How do the promoters of open learning hope to break the barriers that may be putting you off ordinary courses? They usually do it by reducing, or cutting out, the need to attend regular classes.

Self-teaching packages

Instead, they base the learning on self-teaching packages. Such packages consist of some combination of workbooks and other texts, audio-tapes, video-tapes and maybe computers and other equipment. They put across the pre-recorded teaching of a teacher whom you will probably never meet.

The package will usually be backed up by human contact — with a tutor, for example, and with other learners. But the human contact will be small compared with that in normal courses. Most of your learning will come from the package, not from other people. You may not even meet your supporters. Your tutor, for example, may be a friendly voice on the telephone or someone who writes to you about the assignments you send off every couple of weeks.

Such package-based courses can, in theory, open new opportunities to you. They can give you more choice about how to fit learning into your life.

People in the open learning business often judge the openness of a course by asking:

* WHICH ASPECTS of it are more open than usual?

  and

* HOW OPEN are they?

Most programmes labelled as "open" or "flexible" or "distance" learning do offer more opportunities than most "ordinary" courses. But none of them is totally open — and different programmes will be more or less open in different ways.

You may find the following checklist helpful. You can use it to check out an open learning programme and decide whether it really does have the kind of openness you are looking for. It shows what you might call the **extremes** of open/closed on each of a number of aspects. Remember, though, that a given course may lie **between** the extremes on any of these aspects. That is, learners may be given some, but not total choice.

If you are doing a learning programme at the moment, or have finished one recently, try running it through the checklist. On each aspect, are you more inclined to tick the "OPEN" or the "CLOSED" box?

Can I be a learner?

☐ OPEN: Anyone can enrol for the scheme.

☐ CLOSED: It is available only to people of the "right" age, sex, educational qualifications, previous work experience/grade, etc.

Can I suit my own purposes?

☐ OPEN: You can take the course for your own reasons, to suit your own purposes.

☐ CLOSED: The course is chosen for you by someone else, e.g. your employer.

What will I learn?

☐ OPEN: You will choose the content, both by selecting the package and by ignoring material you don't need.

☐ CLOSED: You will need to study the complete course as it is presented to you.

What route can I follow?

☐ OPEN: You can decide your own route.

☐ CLOSED: There is a set route which all must follow.

How will I learn?

☐ OPEN: You will learn from a variety of teaching methods.

☐ CLOSED: The course uses only one teaching method.

Where can I learn?

☐ OPEN: You can learn anywhere you like.

☐ CLOSED: You will have to learn in one set place.

When can I learn?

☐ OPEN: You can learn any day, any time that suits you.

☐ CLOSED: You must learn at certain fixed times.

When can I start and finish?

☐ OPEN: You can start and finish at any time you like.

☐ CLOSED: There is a fixed start and finish time.

At what pace can I learn?

☐ OPEN: You can set your own pace.

☐ CLOSED: The course has a fixed pace.

How will my learning be assessed?

☐ OPEN: You can choose when and how you will be assessed.

☐ CLOSED: You will be assessed at fixed dates by a standard method.

From whom may I get help with my learning?

☐ OPEN: You will be able to choose from a range of people offering different sorts of help.

☐ CLOSED: Only limited help will be available, and from a person chosen for you.

How do you feel on balance about the programme you have just been thinking of? Is it open enough for you? If not, in which aspects do you think it ought to be more open? Jot your reactions in the box opposite.

Learners differ as to where they most want openness. You may, for example, be happy to let someone else decide what is to be learned, so long as you are free to learn it at your own chosen pace. You may be willing to attend a group session in the next town once a fortnight but dig in your heels at the suggestion of attending a week-long residential workshop once a year. We'll all have our different priorities.

The people who market open learning make several big claims for it. They say, in particular, that open learning schemes are about:

- making learning more accessible;
- putting learners' needs and wishes first; and
- helping learners take responsibility for their own learning.

If you've already been involved with an open learning scheme, you may have your own ideas about such claims. Reading this book should help you decide how far the programmes you come across really do adapt to your needs and wishes rather than expecting you to fit in with the demands of the programme and its assessment scheme.

Design your own learning programme

So, let's say you like the sound of open learning. And since it's supposed to be learner-centred — satisfying **your** needs — you may want to specify exactly what form you'd like your programme to take. You can set out the MUST-HAVES and NO-NOs that make clear your personal preferences. It really is important to be clear about what you want — or you may find yourself launched on an unsuitable programme.

Whether you'll find a programme that entirely matches your design is another matter, however. If you want to master brain surgery in two weeks on your kitchen table, for example, even open learning may be unable to oblige. However, if you are willing to be reasonable, and make some compromises, open learning is more likely to satisfy more of your preferences than certain other forms of learning.

All right, let's assume you have a broad idea of:

- what you want to study — e.g. German for importers and exporters, care of the elderly, psychology to degree level;

- how much time you'll be willing to spend on it — days, weeks, years; and

- how much money you will be able to find for it — anything from a few pounds for a self-study course with no tuition to a few thousand pounds for a taught higher degree.

What's your ideal? Now you are looking for a suitable open learning programme. What for you would be the ideal form of programme? Which of the following ingredients would you regard as vital (V), which as acceptable (A) and which as definitely not acceptable (N)?:

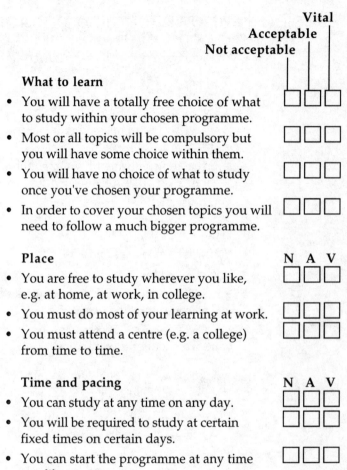

Vital
Acceptable
Not acceptable

What to learn

- You will have a totally free choice of what to study within your chosen programme.
- Most or all topics will be compulsory but you will have some choice within them.
- You will have no choice of what to study once you've chosen your programme.
- In order to cover your chosen topics you will need to follow a much bigger programme.

Place

N A V

- You are free to study wherever you like, e.g. at home, at work, in college.
- You must do most of your learning at work.
- You must attend a centre (e.g. a college) from time to time.

Time and pacing

N A V

- You can study at any time on any day.
- You will be required to study at certain fixed times on certain days.
- You can start the programme at any time you like.
- You can complete it as quickly or as slowly as you please.
- There will be fixed start and finish dates.
- There will be no deadlines to meet as you work through it.
- There will be deadlines to help you keep up the momentum.
- You will be able to negotiate deadlines to suit you.
- You will be able to study in work time.

Learning methods

N A V

- You will learn chiefly from print. ☐☐☐
- You will learn chiefly from television and audio materials. ☐☐☐
- You will learn chiefly from other media, e.g. computers. ☐☐☐
- You will be able to meet other learners informally if you want to. ☐☐☐
- You will be able to attend group learning sessions with other learners if you want to. ☐☐☐
- You must attend such sessions. ☐☐☐

Tutor support

N A V

- You will be able to phone a tutor for help. ☐☐☐
- You will be able to meet a tutor face-to-face. ☐☐☐
- You will be expected to carry out work that will be commented on by a tutor. ☐☐☐
- You will be able to get comments on your work from a tutor if you so wish. ☐☐☐

Assessment

N A V

- Your learning will not be assessed. ☐☐☐
- Your learning will be assessed through essays and other course work. ☐☐☐
- Your learning will be assessed on the basis of your practical performance. ☐☐☐
- Your learning will be assessed by a formal test or examination. ☐☐☐
- Your learning will be assessed against some published standard. ☐☐☐
- You have to reach a certain standard to stay in the programme. ☐☐☐
- Your learning will count towards a certificate or qualification. ☐☐☐
- You will be able to get credit for your existing experience and learning before you begin. ☐☐☐

Do you have other MUST-HAVEs or NO-NOs that I haven't mentioned above? If so write them in the box:

We can never get all we want in any one learning programme. We usually have to compromise on some ingredient or other. For instance, if you are not prepared to wait for a certain programme to begin, then you may be limiting your choice of what to study. And if you want tutors' comments or certification you may have to meet deadlines. But open learning should enable you to find a suitable programme with fewer compromises than you'd normally have to make.

You've now had a chance to think through some of the ways in which open learning programmes can differ. No two are alike in how much freedom they give you to learn in your own way. So keep your preferences in mind. You may want to refer to them (or revise them) later on — especially in Chapter 5 where we look into choosing an open learning programme.

Reflection box

Look back at the objectives at the beginning of this chapter. Do you feel reasonably confident about them? What is the most useful thing you've got from this chapter? How can you apply it? (Make your notes in the box overleaf.)

Follow-up activities

1. Talk with other open learners if you can find some. Ask them how satisfied they are with the openness of their programmes. Which aspects are satisfactory, and which are not? How can you learn from their experience?

2. Send off for details of programmes from the major suppliers, e.g. Open University, National Extension College, Open College. (Their addresses and others are at the back of this book.) How would their programmes suit you in terms of subject-matter and openness?

Chapter 4

How does
open learning work?

Open learning contains nothing unfamiliar. It simply combines existing teaching media and techniques in a new and effective way. This chapter tells you how the teaching works and what it's like to learn from.

Objectives:

When you have worked through this chapter you should be better able to:

- Name the teaching media most often used in open learning packages.

- Give examples of what each medium might do for you that others can't.

- Recognize some of the special teaching techniques used in open learning packages.

- Say what each technique is meant to do for you as a learner.

- Begin thinking about the kind of support you would like to have from human beings while doing your open learning.

The media and what they offer you

Open learning isn't a wildly revolutionary kind of learning. It simply takes a number of teaching approaches that have worked well in separate situations and puts them together in a new way so that you can learn even more from them.

So you will do your open learning chiefly through a learning "package". This will consist of media like printed books, audio-tapes, videos, etc. But a vital part of your learning may come from comments on your work that you get from a tutor. You may or may not be meeting your tutor, and perhaps other learners, in occasional face-to-face sessions.

The diagram below shows how your learning from the various package components on one side might be supported by a variety of human beings on the other. (This chapter deals largely with the left-hand side of this diagram and Chapter 8 with the right.)

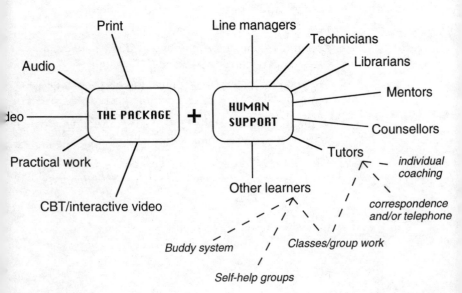

Making the package

Open learning packages are usually produced by a team of people. The team may include:

- an expert in the subject being written about
- one or more teachers or trainers skilled in the various open learning media and techniques
- an editor
- a designer.

Piloting

All of the material is likely to go through several drafts, gathering comments and suggestions from other experts along the way. These experts can comment on the accuracy and relevance of the content; but they can only guess at what learners might make of it. So, before the material is made widely available, it needs to be tried out on some learners who are new to the subject. This is called "developmental testing" or "piloting" in the trade. The purpose of this testing is to find out what learners feel about it and how well they learn from it. The developers will then make whatever improvements seem necessary before it is finally published.

Workbooks

Most open learners do most of their learning from specially prepared workbooks. These are exactly what the name suggests — books that you work with. You must read in order to learn But they are also books that you work IN. Most open learning workbooks have wide margins and plenty of other space left on the pages for you to write down your own ideas. This book you are reading now gives you a bit of space to write in. But most open learning workbooks use A4 format — so the page area is more than twice as big as in this book.

In what ways might you expect to benefit by getting most of your teaching in the form of a book — rather than in class or from other media ? Make a note in the box overleaf:

There are all sorts of benefits you may have mentioned
— e.g. control, cheapness, portability, and maybe the
fact that you are used to learning from print.

The typical open learning workbook builds in a number
of features that you wouldn't expect to see in a run-of-
the-mill textbook or training manual. These include:

• friendly language

• helpful layout

• learning objectives

• activities for the reader to carry out

• links to other media

• frequent summaries

• self-tests, and so on.

I'll say more about some of these later in this chapter.

Some open learning packages also include printed
materials that are already generally available — e.g.
textbooks, reference works, pamphlets, collections of
articles, maps, etc. For instance, a package on disease
in cattle may contain a standard reference manual,
newspaper articles, and leaflets issued by the Ministry
of Agriculture, Fisheries and Food and by the
Agricultural Training Board.   But such a package will
still depend on a workbook designed to help learners
find their way through the rest of the print material.

Audio-cassettes

Sound can be a very powerful medium in open learning. In the early years of the Open University, radio was the chief means of delivering it. Nowadays, however, open learning teachers are making far more use of the audio-cassette. This is because the audio-cassette is much more user-friendly. You don't have to be sitting by your radio at fixed times — often at dawn in the case of Open University broadcasts. You can listen whenever it suits you — and you can hear the material again and again, as often as you please.

And there are more advantages. You don't need to just sit and listen to the teacher who is talking to you on the tape. Right at your finger-tips you have a stop or pause switch — and a rewind switch. So you can make your teacher shut up if you want to think for a minute or two (or pour a cup of coffee). And you can make them repeat what they've said as often as you need to hear it — until you are sure you understand. How often can learners do this to their teacher in a conventional classroom?

There are three main ways of using audio in an open learning package:

- **Just listening**. Talks, discussions, interviews, acted scenes, natural sounds — stuff you can learn from even when your eyes and hands are busy with other things, e.g., while driving a car or washing dishes.

- **Listening and looking**. Here you have to use your eyes as well as your ears. You get printed material to use along with the audio-tape. It may contain diagrams, photographs, maps, charts, tables of figures, etc. which the audio will talk you through.

- **Listening, looking and doing**. Sometimes the audio-teacher may ask you to stop the tape and write something in your workbook, or carry out some practical work with materials and equipment, or with other people. When you switch on again the teacher will comment on what you've done.

But what's so special about audio-teaching? Think of the subject you are interested in. Or think of what you might expect from me if I'd provided an audio-cassette to go with this book. What might you hope to get from an audio-cassette that you couldn't get so easily from a printed workbook?

I asked a number of open learning teachers why they use audio. Here are some of the things they said. Tick any of them that tie in with what you thought you'd be looking for:

- ☐ To provide a welcome relief from reading.
- ☐ To present new ideas to learners who don't care for reading.
- ☐ To help you make best use of your time by giving you a means of learning while doing other things.
- ☐ To talk you through tasks like studying a map or a table of figures — where you might find it distracting to have to keep turning aside to look at written guidance.
- ☐ To help you practise skills.
- ☐ To make the teaching more human and personal.
- ☐ To say things that aren't so easily expressed in print.
- ☐ To encourage or motivate you.
- ☐ To touch your feelings and attitudes.
- ☐ To bring you the voices of people who would be unable or unwilling to say anything in writing.
- ☐ To provide "source material" (e.g. excerpts from an interview) for you to analyse or react to.

Open learners generally speak well of audio-teaching. Here is what some have told me:

- *"It's like having your tutor in the room with you."*
- *"I get more sense out of the books now because I can hear the author's voice in my mind as I read."*
- *"The tapes are alive — they've got warmth and personality — and they cheer me up when the bookwork is getting a bit much."*

One sad note, in passing: There's no evidence that audio-tapes can teach you languages while you sleep.

Video

You may find yourself watching television as part of your open learning programme. If you are doing an Open University undergraduate course, the material may be broadcast to you by the BBC. But with many Open University courses, and most courses from other providers that use television, the material will come on video-cassette. In the same way as audio-cassettes, videos are more user-friendly — provided, of course, you've got access to a playback machine.

Video adds an extra dimension to learning. You can have pictures in workbooks and sound from an audio-tape. But a video brings you **moving** pictures (and in full colour). And the sound — which may be people talking or music or voice-over commentary — ties in with those moving pictures to give you a sense of "being there" that is difficult for other media to match.

I asked a number of open learning teachers why they used video. They mentioned a number of uses which I've listed below. Which of them might be helpful to you in the subject(s) you want to learn?

 To show you how to use tools or equipment.

To demonstrate skills that you may be learning — e.g. interviewing or car-driving.

To take you through the stages of a procedure — e.g. a science experiment or a manufacturing process.

☐ To present a dramatic or musical performance — if it is important to see as well as hear the performers.

☐ To analyse change over time, using animation, freeze-frame, slow-motion or speeded-up pictures — e.g. the movements of an animal or the growth of a plant.

☐ To convey the three-dimensional qualities of an object — e.g. a building or a piece of sculpture — by moving the camera around it.

☐ To show a discussion or interaction between two or more people in which "body language" is important.

☐ To take you into situations — e.g. into an intensive care unit or the cockpit of an aircraft about to land — which you might not otherwise be able to enter.

☐ To provide source material for you to explore or analyse, using principles or techniques taught in the course — e.g. a recording of scenes of violence at a football match.

☐ To help you feel with the people in a certain situation — e.g. with hospital patients or victims of crime.

I hope this will have given you some ideas about how you might learn from video material. If you're still not sure, you might find it interesting to watch one or two broadcast programmes and see whether they have any of the effects mentioned in the list above. Look out particularly for Open University programmes or for any "educational" broadcasts that have "fact sheets" you can send off for.

Practical kits

If you are learning practical skills you may well need to practice with equipment or materials. You may be able to do this in a college laboratory or a firm's workshop. If not, the course authors will have to provide all the necessary materials in a practical kit you can use at home. For instance, a helium neon-laser for producing holograms was necessary in one course I remember. Other practical kits I know of have included items like refrigeration piping, electronic circuit boards and even a robot.

Needless to say, the practical kits won't help you much on their own. You need guidance on what to do with them. You'll normally get this from a printed workbook, but sometimes you may get an audio-cassette to talk you through the practical work.

Computers   Many people take up open learning nowadays in order to learn about computers. What better way to learn about computers, you might think, than to learn **from** a computer. Packages in this area will naturally use the computer itself as the main teaching medium.

But there are computer-based packages on many other subjects — like engineering design or preparing a budget. This is because the computer will allow learners to do things faster, or more realistically, or with greater understanding than if they were using paper and pencil exercises alone. This approach is usually called CBT — computer-based training, or sometimes CAL — computer-assisted learning.

CBT or CAL can be used in a variety of ways to help you learn. Their biggest strength lies in being able to show you different material according to what **you** type on the computer keyboard. For instance, you can tell the computer to alter diagrams or tables of figures on the screen. Similarly, if you make mistakes in answering questions the computer has put to you, it will be able to tell you immediately where you have gone wrong. So you can interact with the medium in a way that you can't with a book.

Interactive   A computer can also be combined with video to give
video   you "interactive video". Here, at various key points in the teaching, different learners will get different pictures and sound from their TV monitors depending on what they have tapped into the computer keyboard.

If you've already used CBT or CAL, what do you like best and least about it? If you haven't, how do you feel about the idea of using it?

Many learners find it easier to concentrate with computers than they do with workbooks and other media. And they get a kind of feedback that other media cannot give. But there is the snag that you can't always work on the package at a time and place to suit yourself as perhaps you can with other media. And some CBT packages are not very interactive — so what they give you could get more easily from a book.

By the way, you don't have to be "computer-literate" before you start on CBT. So if you're not, and you find it's part of your programme, have no fear. The package itself will tell you anything you need to know as you go along.

How do packages teach?

In one sense, packages don't teach. Like I said in the title of this book, you teach yourself — with the help of a package. But in another sense packages do teach. Somewhere, sometime — maybe hundreds of miles away and many months ago — a human teacher toiled over blank sheets of paper or an equally blank computer screen, sweating out the words and images that must somehow do for you what that teacher would do if she or he could be by your side when you are ready to learn. When you open your package you release that teacher from a sort of suspended animation. He or she is instantly at your service.

Your ideal teacher?

So what do you expect the teacher-in-your-package to do in order to help you learn? Probably much the same as you'd expect of any other ideal teacher. I've started listing a few of my expectations below. Perhaps you would like to add some more of your own to the list.

My ideal teacher would:

- Give me a clear idea of where we are going.
- Explain things clearly.
- Allow me time to practise.

What would **you** expect of an ideal teacher?:

Here is my list continued. Have you mentioned anything I've missed? (My ideal teacher would...)

- Be friendly and approachable.
- Use plain, everyday language.
- Use helpful examples (including pictures).
- Explain things clearly — and in more than one way.
- Realize I need frequent breaks.
- Give me a chance to draw on my own experience.
- Help me apply what I am learning to my situation.

- Summarize the main points from time to time.
- Help me to check my own progress.
- Give me guidance on how to do better.

Teaching techniques

Most of us expect quite a lot from a good teacher. And we must expect quite as much from a good open learning package. But can a package carry out tasks like those we've listed above? Yes, it can. We can show this by looking at an open learning workbook. The writer of an open learning workbook uses a number of techniques meant to help you learn.

These techniques aren't often found in ordinary textbooks and training manuals. But they are often found not only in open learning workbooks but **also** in open learning videos and audio material and in computer teaching.

If you've examined any open learning materials, you may know of these techniques already. I expect you've also noticed that I am using some of the teaching techniques of open learning in this book.

Have a quick skim through the pages of this book — and look especially at the sample pages from workbooks at the end of this chapter. See if you can pick out three or four things that you don't normally find in a textbook — special tricks of the trade that authors use to help readers learn. Note them below:

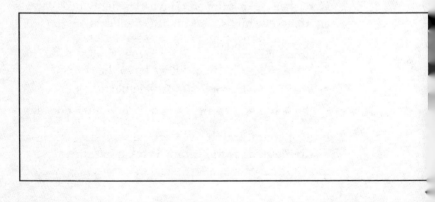

Here are some of the techniques I've used or which you may have noticed in the sample pages at the end of the chapter. Did you spot any helpful techniques that are **not** on my list?

- Objectives.
- Friendly, "You" & "I" style of writing
- Shortish chunks of learning.
- Fewer words than usual per page.
- Plenty of examples.
- Ideas offered by other learners.
- Illustrations where they are better than words.
- Headings to help you find your way around.
- Links to other media. (I sometimes suggest you discuss things with other learners.)
- Relating what I'm writing about to your needs.
- Chances for you to apply the ideas we are talking about.
- Space for you to write down your own ideas.

I'll now say a bit more about some of these features because you may want to look for them in choosing an open learning package. Unless a package uses them properly it probably won't be much good to you.

Objectives

Most authors of open learning workbooks will make clear what the objectives are. You'll usually find they have listed the objectives for the whole course or programme at the beginning of the workbook, or in a separate study guide. In addition they may tell you the objectives for each separate section of the course, section by section, as you work through.

Objectives tell you what you should be able to DO as a result of your learning. All learning should enable us to talk about the world in new ways and/or to act upon it in new ways. For instance, suppose you were studying an open learning package called *Diet and Nutrition*. Its objectives might be that you should be able to:

- **List** the important components of food.

- **State** what each component provides for the body.

- **Give examples** of foodstuffs in which each component is found.

- **Interpret** food composition tables.

- **Calculate** the quantity of components in sample diets.

- **Recognize** the factors determining a person's dietary needs.

- **Interpret** tables of recommended dietary intake.

- **Evaluate** sample diets against recommended dietary intake.

- **Plan** a balanced diet for given individuals.

Notice the words in bold that say what you are learning to DO.

What are you learning to do in this section of this book at the moment? Jot down your idea of what the objectives might be **before** you look back to check the ones I listed at the beginning of the chapter.

This section of the chapter is particularly meant to help you achieve the third and fourth objective I listed at the beginning of the chapter. Do you feel you're getting there?

With most textbooks, and many classes, you're never told what you're supposed to get out of them. With open learning you are. Once you know what you are learning to do, you are in a better position to assess your own progress towards that goal. You don't have to depend entirely on someone else telling you how you are getting on. At the end of a package, or a section within it, you should be able to look back at each objective and say: "Can I now do that to my satisfaction?" I hope you are doing that in the Reflection Boxes as you work through this book.

Objectives don't apply just to workbooks. Suppose you are listening to an audio-tape or watching a video, or doing some practical work or computer-based training. It still pays to ask the same question: "What should I be able to do as a result of this? What are the objectives?"

Activities

"Activities" are perhaps the most visible feature of open learning materials. They take the form of questions or suggestions for you to do something. They may be signalled in various ways. For instance:

- In some texts they are labelled "Activity" or "Self-assessment Question (SAQ)".

- In others there is no label but just a symbol alongside — perhaps a fancy letter A or a hand holding a pencil.

- *In yet other texts, you can easily spot the activities because they are printed in a different COLOUR or a different style of type.* Or maybe (as in this book) they have a blank space for you to write in.

- Sometimes there will be a rule of type across the page — to encourage you to stop and do the activity before reading on. For example:

❀❀❀

Activities take different forms. They also ask you to do different things and may take different amounts of time. Some will simply ask you to read through a

checklist and tick off the items you agree with. Some
will ask you to write down your first thoughts on a
topic. Such exercises may take only a few seconds of
your time. But others will take longer. In some
subjects you may need to think something out, or draw
a diagram or work out some figures.

You may even be asked to get up and leave your
package — to go and do something at work, around
the home, or in the community. You may be asked to
interview some colleagues, to observe what goes on in
the local magistrates' court or to keep notes on how
your children answer when you ask them about school.
It all depends what is right for the subject you are
learning about. With activities of this sort, you may
spend longer on them than on reading the package.

What are activities for? Let's make an activity out of
this question. In the space below, write down one
reason why you think an author might put activities
into an open learning package:

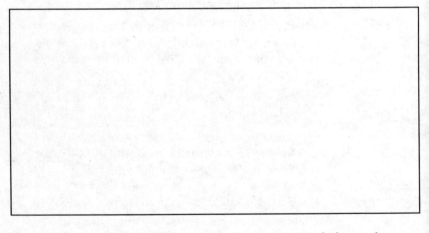

The overall purpose of activities is to help you learn.
But the list opposite shows in more detail why authors
use them. Obviously, no one activity will have all
these purposes at once. In fact, not all of these
purposes will show up within every package.

You may like to use the list to check through the activities in this book and in the sample pages. What purposes does each activity seem to have? Tick off each purpose you can find examples of. What, for a start, is the purpose of the activity you've just done?

Activities may be meant to help you:

- [ ] remember the ideas in the package
- [ ] understand the ideas in the package
- [ ] make use of the ideas in the package
- [ ] think for yourself
- [ ] learn by doing
- [ ] bring in your own experience and examples
- [ ] reflect on your own thoughts and feelings
- [ ] obtain information that the package cannot provide
- [ ] apply your learning to your work or personal life
- [ ] practise towards important objectives
- [ ] monitor your own progress
- [ ] identify your strengths and weaknesses
- [ ] keep a record of what you have done.

I expect you'll have found activities with most of those purposes. Ideally there will be some variety among the activities in a package. If they're all of the same sort, you may feel less inclined to do them. And you might miss something important as a result. (The chief purpose of this activity, by the way, was to help you understand the idea of activities. And the previous one aimed to get you to think for yourself.)

Feedback

We all need feedback in order to learn. Feedback is anything that tells us about the results of our actions, perhaps allowing us to do differently next time. For instance, if we're learning to change gears in a car, the physical reaction of the car itself is one form of feedback. Another comes from our driving instructor — who tells us we've got it right or, if not, why not.

Feedback is an important feature of an open learning
package. You'll notice that activities in a workbook
are usually followed by some sort of information that
helps you think again about what you have done.
Sometimes this is placed immediately after the
activity. Sometimes it is put on a later page — so that
you don't catch sight of it before you do the activity.

Feedback may take various forms. For instance, the
author may give you:

- the correct answer if there is one

- sample answers if more than one is possible

- responses that have been made by other learners

- advice as to how you can assess your own answer

- questions about what you learned from the activity

- sympathy about difficulties you may have had

- reassurance about possible errors you may have
  fallen into.

In general, the author is trying to help you assess what
you have done and perhaps compare your thoughts
with those of the author or other people. It can
sometimes be very frustrating to spend time on an
activity if the author doesn't feed you back some
relevant comments. For instance, you may feel left in
the dark as to whether you are working on the right
lines. Or you may say "So what?" — because you don't
see where the activity leads.

There will be times when the activity provides its own
feedback or you get some sort of feedback from outside
the text. If you are doing practical work, like wiring a
3-pin plug on a table lamp, the result you get will tell
you whether you've carried it out correctly. The lamp
either lights or it doesn't. (Though the thoughtful
author may still give you feedback in the form of a list
of things to check again if your lamp fails to light up.)

Again, some activities may suggest you take what you have done — e.g. a plan you have outlined — and discuss it with other people. Their comments will act as feedback. That is, they should help you reflect on what you have learned and what you might do next.

How do you feel about the feedback I've been giving after activities in this book?

Naturally, I don't know what you've said. So I can't comment on it. The only thing I can feed back to you here is my hope that you generally find my comments to be reasonably helpful. What can you do if you feel the feedback to some activities is less than satisfactory? Apart from cursing the author, one thing you might do is discuss those activities with other people — e.g. a friend or a tutor. They may be able to give you just the feedback you need.

Self-tests Packages often include self-tests to help you measure your progress against all the objectives so far. These will usually be a set of questions with the feedback printed somewhere in the package. Sometimes they may be "computer marked" (multiple-choice) questions and you must send off your answers to get feedback.

Examples   Good open learning materials will include plenty of
examples. The best teachers have always known that
people may have difficulty with abstract ideas. We
often don't really grasp what the experts are trying to
tell us until they give us a "for instance".

You want an example of what I am talking about right
now? Well, take the parables of Jesus. He knew better
than to lecture on ethical and theological principles.
Instead he told stories about people like his listeners —
and these stories demonstrated the principles. They
brought the ethics and theology to life. Here, of
course, I'm assuming that you have at least some idea
of what the parables were like. If you don't (and a lot
of people don't nowadays) then you won't be much
wiser. Even my example will need an example.

Your open learning programme will probably be full of
new ideas, new theories and new methods. They will
all be capable of altering the way you see the world
and the way you operate in it. But only if you can see
how they apply. And this will depend to a large extent
on whether the author has provided examples that
show how the ideas work out in real life.

Examples may take several forms: e.g.

- references to things you already know (e.g. the
  parables of Jesus)

- anecdotes, stories and case studies

- pictures (photographs, diagrams, maps, etc)

- audio and video material

- real objects (e.g. rock specimens or fabric swatches)

- graphs or charts and tables of figures

- calculations showing all the steps to a solution

- quotations from other people

- examples provided by other learners

- examples you provide from your own experience
  (probably in response to an activity).

What kinds of example would you hope to find in the subject you are studying (or intend to study)?

As you'll have noticed, I have just asked you for examples of the final kind mentioned in the list above. That is, I asked you to think of your own examples.

Obviously, different subjects will call for different kinds of examples. If any parts of your package contained the wrong sorts of examples, or not enough, you might find it lifeless and dull. In that case, you might need to discuss it with someone else — a friend or a tutor — and try to find examples of your own.

Signals

The designers of learning materials usually give a lot of thought to layout and graphics. But they're not just trying to pretty up the pages. They are using **signals** meant to help you find your way around the package and know what's going on. For instance:

- **White space**. The pages of open learning workbooks are usually less crowded than other texts — so as to focus your attention (and avoid intimidating you).

- **Headings**. Big headings are used to break up the text into manageable chunks and also to give you an idea of what each chunk is about. Smaller headings within each chunk give you more detail.

- **Bulleted lists**. Lists (like this one) are often better than solid text for showing a number of related points. "Bullets" (•) or other devices (~) may be used to make them stand out more clearly.

- **Boxes**. Certain kinds of text — e.g. quotations or interesting side-issues — may be put in boxes as a reminder that you're meant to pay it a different kind of attention.

- **Symbols**. Symbols in the margin are often used to tell you what sort of material you are about to deal with. The symbols alongside, for example, are the sort that might be used to indicate (in order):

    ~ an activity
    ~ practical work
    ~ using a video
    ~ using audio material
    ~ referring to other printed material
    ~ follow-up work
    ~ an assignment to be sent to a tutor.

Obviously, different packages use such signals in different ways. If you familiarize yourself with how they are being used in any new package you pick up, then you'll find your way around in it more easily.

Which of the five different kinds of signal can you find examples of in this book — or in the sample pages? Can you see any other kinds of signals being used?

No feedback this time— I'll let you provide your own.

So what's it like to learn from?

Learning from a well-made package is like having a good human coach or tutor, working with you one-to-one. Good human tutors will tell you what you are expected to get out of a session. They will present you with clear explanations and examples that tie in to your experience. They will give you frequent opportunities to apply the ideas being discussed and see how much progress you have made. They may suggest ways you can learn from other people. They will offer comments that help you review what you have done.

Experts have said that a good open learning package is like "a tutorial-in-print". The average package may not be as good as one-to-one teaching from the best live tutors in the world. But most of us can't get one-to-one teaching anyway. And if we did, it might not be from the best tutors in the world. So, an ideal compromise might be a high quality package for basic learning — plus help from a real tutor where we most need it.

Human support

Open learning isn't just packages. There's a great deal you can learn from a well-made package. But you'll learn yet more if you can get help from some real live human beings. However good it is, the package is pre-recorded teaching. It has to do all things for all learners. It can't respond to your individual needs. It can't answer your questions. It can't give you yet another explanation when you still don't understand. It can't look over your shoulder while you make your first attempt at some tricky practical task. It can't cheer you up when you feel you are not learning as fast as you want to. These are things that can be done only by other people.

However, you may not need to suffer the loneliness of the long-distance learner. You may be able to get support from other people while you work through your open learning programme. In fact, this can be so important to success in open learning that I have devoted the whole of Chapter 8 to it.

Reflection box

Look back at the objectives at the beginning of this chapter. Do you feel reasonably confident about them? What is the most important thing you've got from this chapter? How might you apply it?

Follow-up activities

1. Read Chapter 8 (if you haven't already) for the "human side" of what makes open learning work.
2. Find some other open learners, if you can, and ask them what they think about the way open learning works for them.

Sample pages from open learning workbooks

Sources
The nine sample pages that follow are from open learning workbooks produced by the following organizations and are reprinted here with their kind permission:

A. Capel Manor Open Learning Unit— from a course for staff in garden centres.

B. National Extension College — from a course on business administration.

C. Open University — from a course on fluid mechanics.

D. Open University — from a course on the 19th century novel.

E. Open University — from a course on technology.

F. Open College — from a course for managers.

G. Open College — from a course on electronics.

N.B. The originals were all A4 in size, and some were printed in more than one colour.

Common features
I'm not suggesting that these pages are typical of what you will find in open learning workbooks. Indeed, you'll see that they differ quite a lot among themselves. But I think you'll find they have certain features in common — features you might not expect to find in the normal textbook or training manual. (I list some of these on page 47.)

Questions
You may well have no interest at all in any of the subjects dealt with in these sample pages. That shouldn't matter. Just ask yourself: "What is the author doing to help the reader learn?" and "Might I find that sort of approach helpful in **my** subject?" This should help you later in choosing a package.

A

Section 1: Why trees and shrubs, and how to find out more about them

In this Section I'll look at why some gardeners prefer trees and shrubs to more formal garden designs. I'll also show you how to make a 'Looking good' list of plants for each month and how to collect information about each plant so that you can make sound recommendations to your customers.

Why choose trees and shrubs?

Many knowledgeable gardeners prefer to have borders that contain mixed shrubs rather than complex bedding designs and herbaceous borders. Why do you think this is? Try to think of 3 reasons and jot them down in the box below.

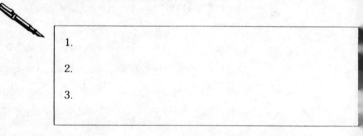

1.

2.

3.

You could have suggested any of the following reasons:

1. Trees and shrubs offer an attractive, year-round display, with a variety of form, colour and height. The careful selection of plants will ensure:

    • something is in flower all year round (see the section in **Hillier's Manual of Trees & Shrubs**, page 567, and pages 33, 37 and 44 of **The Tree & Shrub Expert**)
    • a contrast of colour (variegated or evergreen leaves) and shape (bold-shaped foliage or fern-like leaves)
    • berries or stems for winter colour.

2. A mixture of shrubs can cover the ground so as to suppress weed growth.

3. Digging is unnecessary once trees and shrubs are established, and only light cultivation is needed. Read the articles on mulching and hoeing on page 107 of **The Tree & Shrub Expert**.

4. Pruning is generally straightforward – many trees and shrubs only require pruning to keep them within bounds.

5. Once planted, the border is permanent.

6. Trees and shrubs give the garden an informal, natural and mature look.

7. Shrubs enable the garden to be divided up with colourful and attractive plants (rather than a formal hedge). They can hide or disguise ugly corners or features.

The range of tree and shrub species and varieties available to the British gardener is colossal. Many are quite common, and are sold in most garden centres and planted in gardens and public open spaces. Don't despise a plant just because it is common; many of the finest and most attractive trees and shrubs belong to this popular group – a large proportion of your turnover will be from these plants.

Your 'Looking good' lists

Each month I'll ask you to choose 5 plants that are 'looking good' and to collect information about each one in your notebook. (I'll explain later how to arrange this information in your notebook.)

How do you decide which plants 'look good'?

The plants you choose will be those that have a particularly attractive feature that month. The most obvious feature would be a showy display of flowers, but there are others. Try to jot down 2 more below.

1.

2.

B

The reception area

Start this section by carrying out the following activity which will help you assess
what makes a good reception area.

ACTIVITY 7 Look at the following picture of a receptionist and reception area. This is not an
ideal situation. What is wrong with it? Label the bad points shown in the picture.

Turn to page 36 for our assessment of this reception area. Look, too, at the
picture on page 23 which offers a real contrast – a much more welcoming and
attractive scene!

C

two surfaces. The surfaces are inclined so that the fluid can build up a high pressure which can be used to support very large loads. The gap between the slider and bearing is small ($\simeq 2.5 \times 10^{-2}$ mm) compared to the length of the slider ($\simeq 150$ mm).

These examples show the importance of knowing the important physical features in a problem, and illustrate the limitations of the mathematical model when solving a fluid mechanics problem.

Before attempting the following end-of-section exercise, read the summary of the section given in the Handbook.

End-of-section Exercise

Solution on p. 42

(a) Classify the following statements as true or false.

    (i)   A fluid cannot remain at rest if a shearing force is applied.

    (ii)   Shearing forces cause continuous and permanent distortion of fluids.

    (iii) Gases are fluids.

    (iv) Liquids are not fluids.

    (v)   Gases and liquids are both fluids.

    (vi) A fluid may be either a gas or a liquid.

    (vii) A gas will expand to fill completely its container.

    (viii) A fluid is considered to be incompressible.

    (ix) The molecules of a fluid are more mobile than those of a solid.

(b) Explain the effect of compressional forces and shearing forces on a volume of liquid.

(c) In this section you have seen examples in which the flow of a fluid can be split into 3 regions (for the purpose of modelling): ideal flow region, wake and boundary layer. In which of these regions is viscosity omitted from the model? On what grounds is this step taken?

Section 2   Some Simple Experiments

In this section you will have the opportunity to get your hands wet by doing some simple experiments which illustrate some of the features of fluid flow that will be described in this course. The apparatus for each experiment should be collected together according to the lists given, and the experiments should be carried out while listening to the audio-tape. The tape presenter will describe what features to look out for. Stop and start signals are not used during the experimental sessions, but long pauses have been left to give you time to observe what is happening.

Keep the tape going right through each session.

We do not need complicated equipment to observe fluid flow behaviour; important phenomena can be seen all around the house. For example, we shall begin in the bathroom.

Session 1   You will need:

In the bathroom.

(i)   a bath with approximately 10 centimetres of water in it;

(ii) a ruler;

(iii) a pencil;

(iv) some powder, e.g. talcum powder.

For this experimental session, you will need to be able to listen to your audio-tape recorder in the bathroom. If this is not possible, then you could either make a note of what to look out for, or carry out the experiments in a large bowl of water in the vicinity of your recorder.

In any case, be aware of the danger of water in the presence of an electrical appliance.

When you are ready, start the tape.

D

8   TOLSTOY'S MORAL NEUTRALITY

8.1   'I have found', Tolstoy once said to a friend, 'that a story leaves a deeper impression when it is impossible to tell which side the author is on'. (See p. 45 for the full quotation.) As Tolstoy puts it, this might sound no more than a clever author's device; but I would suggest that it means something deeper.

8.2   Consider the question of 'taking sides' in a novel for a moment. It is surely very important in almost all the novels you have studied in this Course. (You will remember Graham Holderness's remarks about it in connection with *Wuthering Heights*; see Units 4–5). You can put it to yourself in this way: do the authors, at certain points in their novel, depend on your feeling *indignant*, or *gladdened*? Well, clearly, Jane Austen expects you to feel indignant at Mrs Norris's treatment of Fanny; Henry James expects you to feel indignant at Maisie's treatment at the hands of her parents; and George Eliot expects you to be gladdened that Dorothea, at a low point in her own fortunes, has the strength of mind to think of others.

8.3   Or you could put it another way: do the authors expect you to form *wishes*? Does Jane Austen expect you to *want* Fanny to be freed from oppression, and Turgenev expect you to *wish* that Insarov might not be doomed (as he so plainly is). I think you will agree that they do, and that this is the means by which they get you to make certain sorts of judgement for yourself.

Ask yourself, therefore: do you feel indignation, or gladness, or a wish that things could be different in reading *Anna Karenina*?

Discussion

8.4   Let us take indignation. Do you feel indignant, at Karenin's horrible letter to Anna? At Anna's neglect of her daughter? At Oblonsky's misdoings? For myself, I don't think that I do, or that I am meant to. Tolstoy *could* have made us indignant at these things with perfect ease, but it is not part of his plan to do so. Tolstoy places you, as a reader, at a point of vantage where you feel no wish that things should be different.

8.5   Does this mean that he is aloof and indifferent towards the fate of his characters —that he is treating them simply as a spectacle and intends us to do the same?

Discussion

8.6   I would say, not at all. He feels, and makes us feel, intensely for his characters, but this feeling is of a special kind: it is the feeling of kinship, of human solidarity, the sort of bond which unites the species and holds society together. He once wrote in his diary that 'The powerful means to true happiness in life, is to let flow from oneself on all sides, without any laws, like a spider, a cobweb of love, and to catch in it all that comes to hand: women old or young, children, or policemen'.[1] It is a good description of the way he writes; and this spider-like

---

[1] He made this diary-entry on 26 April 1856. (See Aylmer Maude's *Life of Tolstoy*, World's Classics ed., Dent, vol. 1, p. 151.)

E

Activity 1 Your own house's face

The purpose of this activity is to begin a design analysis of your own house, starting from the outside (the 'face' your house presents to you and your neighbours) and, in later activities, working inwards to the plan and other details. (Estimated activity time: about ½-1 hour.)

1   From memory (i.e. do it straight away, without first going outside to look) draw the front of your house. Don't worry about details that you cannot remember, but try to make your drawing as clear and as detailed as you can, although obviously you probably won't be skilled at drawing and your attempt may in fact be fairly 'childish'. Try asking other members of your household to make their own drawings, too, without looking at each other's until you have all finished. (As with all these activities, my own attempt is shown alongside.)

My drawing of the front of our house, from memory

2   Compare your drawings one with another. Are there any large differences between what you each remember and have drawn? Has someone in the family clearly got a better memory of all the details of the front of your house, or do you disagree among yourselves as to the details and their relative locations?

My daughter's drawing of the front of our house, from memory

3   Now go and look at the front of your house and compare the reality with the drawings. Are there any large differences between the reality and what is supposed to be represented on the drawings? Did you have a good visual memory of the front of your house, or have you not really looked carefully at it before? Try making another drawing from observation, to improve on your first attempt.

A photograph of my house (the one in the middle)

F

| UNIT 4 | **THE INTERVIEW** |

Introduction

In this unit you will look at the art of effective interviewing. It sounds easy, but to be a good interviewer takes skill, self discipline and a knowledge of your own prejudices.

Purposes of this unit

When you have completed this unit you should be able to:

- create a suitable environment for an interview
- plan a structure for the discussion
- prepare individual questions based on the seven point plan
- take into consideration the importance of first impressions
- conduct the interview in such a way as to acquire the information needed to come to a fair decision
- close the interview effectively
- make a final decision and take appropriate follow-up action.

1 Why interview?

Interviews are the most common and, sometimes, the sole method by which organisations assess a candidate's suitability for the job.

Since so much depends on these encounters, it is worth asking how effective they are as a means of selection.

What can interviews tell you about a candidate's ability to do a job? – and what can't they tell you?
Write your ideas in the space below:

They can tell you ....

_____

_____

_____

_____

They cannot tell you ...

_____

_____

_____

_____

David, regional manager, clearing bank

'I'm very much in favour of interviews because you meet candidates face to face. I believe you can make an accurate judgement of their interpersonal skills and you have the chance to pose questions which can test this. The other factors are less tangible; you can get a sense of their enthusiasm – perhaps even their approach -- and, most importantly, a sense of how much they want the job.'

Ronnie, distribution manager, sportswear manufacturer

'We use interviews almost exclusively -- other methods are only used for top jobs. I think so much depends on the skills of the interviewer. The best interviewers can draw out much of the information they require, but most of us only interview sporadically. I've also found that interviews rarely help me to answer what for me is a big question: can they do the job in the way we want?'

Gwen, section head, petrochemical company

'My background is in personnel so I suppose I have a slightly different view of interviewing. I believe interviewing is the most effective way of selecting staff for most jobs but I feel it's very easy to have far too much faith in it as a single method. If there is no other method such as testing involved, always try to make sure that the application forms and preparatory work by selectors are as detailed as possible.'

Can you add anything else to the list as a result of what these managers described? After you have finished, compare your list with the one below.

They can tell you about:

- attributes such as appearance and manner

- motivation and how much the candidate wants the job

- interpersonal and communication skills

They can also ...

- enable the candidate to ask questions about the job

- give you the chance to find out more about specific points

They cannot tell you about:

- the candidate's practical skills

Other drawbacks ...

- inexperienced interviewers might not help the candidate to be seen in the best light

- interview nerves may inhibit an otherwise excellent candidate

G

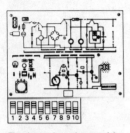

The picture shows the part of the kit you'll be working on — the bridge rectifier circuit. You'll also need your multimeter and two short wire links. Before you start, make sure that you've removed the wire from link LK1 after Practical 6, and check that the fault switches are all in their correct positions.

PRACTICAL WORK

1 Connect up links 3 and 6.

2 Switch on at the mains and at your kit.

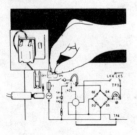

3 Set your multimeter to 20 volts dc and switch it on.

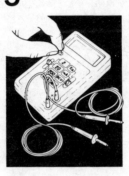

4 Put the black meter probe on test point TP4 and the red probe on test point TP3, and note the voltage reading you get.

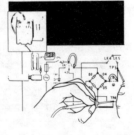

The voltage you just measured was the output voltage of the full-wave bridge rectifier on your kit. It should have been over 8 volts dc, much higher than the voltage you got from the half-wave rectifier. In fact, because the bridge rectifier gives you twice as many pulses as the half-wave rectifier does, its output voltage is about 90 percent of the ac voltage, compared with the 45 percent you get from a half-wave rectifier.

That's the end of the practical work for this unit, so switch off your kit and your meter and put them away safely.

Chapter 5

Choosing your open learning programme

You may think open learning sounds right for you. But how do you find out what's available? Whom do you go to for help? How do you decide whether a particular programme is likely to meet your needs?

Objectives:

When you've worked through this chapter you should be better able to:

- Track down printed information about packages and programmes that may be of use to you.

- Find people who can give you further information and possibly support your learning.

- Weigh up the open learning materials in terms of what they will be offering you and what demands they will make on you.

- Decide whether people offering to support you are likely to give you what you need.

- Agree an open learning programme with a person or organization offering you support.

NOTE: Even if you're being put on a programme rather than choosing one, this chapter may still help you get the best out of that programme.

Who does what in open learning?

You may find it useful to know what goes on in the open learning business. There are three main aspects:

Production: Who produces the package of learning materials that you will be using?

Delivery: Who delivers the learning package — both in terms of selling it to you and in terms of providing tutorial or other support if you want it?

Certification: Who can assess what you have learned from the package and award you a qualification (if applicable)? If your open learning is provided by your employer there may be no certification apart from getting "signed off".

The Open University & others

With some courses, the same organization handles all three aspects. The Open University, for instance, produces courses, delivers the tutorial support and awards degrees, certificates and diplomas to successful learners. Several other universities and colleges have now started doing the same.

National Extension College

The National Extension College delivers and produces. Some of the courses it delivers are developed by the Open University and other producers. But mostly it is delivering courses that it has produced itself. However, it does not offer certification. Its students get their learning certified by such bodies as BTEC, SCOTVEC and the GCSE boards.

The Open College

Another such national provider is the Open College. Some of the courses it delivers it has produced itself, while others are produced by other people.

Delivery agents

Yet other organizations are purely delivery agents. That is, they produce no courses of their own but simply market and support courses produced by other people. Many local FE colleges fall into this category.

If you are taking an open learning course at work then it could be that your employers are delivering someone else's package or they may have produced it in-house.

"So what?" you may say. Why should you care who does what in the world of open learning? Where it matters is in deciding whom to ask for advice and what to make of the kind of advice you get.

If you go to the Open University, you are most likely to get advice about Open University courses. The staff you speak with are likely to know far more about Open University courses than they are about other people's courses that might just happen to suit your needs better. Similarly with staff of the National Extension College and other providers.

Shopping around　On the other hand, if you go to someone who is purely concerned with delivery, you may hear of packages from several producers — but still only from the producers that your chosen deliverer happens to deal with. So, don't be satisfied with just one source of advice. Seek information from more than one producer. And, if possible, go to more than one deliverer. (Remember that neither the producer nor deliverer may be responsible for getting your learning certified; you may need to make your own arrangements — possibly with the deliverer's help.)

Finding out what's available

So what kinds of information do you need? Two things, probably:

1. Can I find a package to suit my needs?

2. Can I find a suitable support service?

Remember that an open learning programme consists of a package plus a support service (like tutoring, and possibly help with certification).

How will you find out about packages and support services? Partly from printed materials, partly by going and talking with people. Here are some suggestions:

Catalogues   Write to or telephone some of the producers, asking for a catalogue of their materials and/or of their courses if they also deliver them. (The addresses and telephone numbers of some of the main producers are listed at the back of this book.)

Perhaps there are other producers you know about who are not on my list but may be worth contacting. If so, jot down their names below to remind yourself:

```



```

There are many other producers catering for learners in different occupational groups — glass, knitting, electrical engineering, and so on. I haven't been able to list them all. But you will probably find most of them listed in the publication I describe below:

Open   Consult a book called *The Open Learning Directory.*
Learning   This is a catalogue of more than 2000 open learning
Directory   packages updated every year. Many large public libraries will have a copy for reference. If they haven't they should be able to obtain one or tell you where you'll find one — perhaps in a local FE college.

The *Directory* is divided into 18 subject areas — from Agriculture through Engineering to Social Welfare. For every package in each subject-area it tells you:

- what the package is about
- who it's for
- what prior learning or qualifications (if any) you need to start on it
- what level the package is at
- what qualification (if any) it leads to
- how long it will take to work through
- what learning materials you get
- what special equipment (if any) you will need
- what it will cost you
- what tutorial support is available (if any)
- who produces the package and/or how to obtain further information about it.

The *Directory* also has a section listing all the publishers (producers) and the main subject categories their packages cover. This may give you further ideas about whom to contact for catalogues.

However, the *Directory* is firmly geared towards training and occupational competence. So you won't find any mention of packages that are more generally educational. No mention, for instance of the GCSE subjects covered by the National Extension College. No mention of the dozens of degree-level courses in literature, music, history, psychology, politics, etc. produced by the Open University.

Getting advice

Sooner or later you may want to speak to someone who delivers open learning. If you don't live too far away, you may visit one of the local centres of the Open College or one of the regional centres of the Open University. (The Open College centres are listed in the *Directory* — but if you can't get hold of a copy you can ask the College for their addresses. The addresses of the Open University regional centres are likewise available from the University.)

You may also decide to visit some other local delivery centre — possibly one that delivers packages from a range of producers. These too are listed in the *Open Learning Directory* — 28 pages of them in the latest edition. Most are local colleges, but a few are private companies. The *Directory* gives details of each including the name of a person to contact.

Local colleges

Whether or not it is listed in the *Directory*, you may want to see what you can find out from your local college. This may go by the name of "college of further education", "college or institute of higher education (or further and higher education)", "tertiary college" or "college of technology". Or perhaps just "college". Many of the "new universities" (formerly polytechnics) also deliver some of their courses by open learning.

Somewhere within any local college you should find someone who knows about open learning opportunities in your area. Even if your college doesn't have an Open Learning Unit or Flexible Learning Centre or some such within it, someone there should know where the nearest one is. If they don't, telephone the local education authority and ask to speak to whoever is responsible for adult education in your area.

Summary+

The list opposite sums up the possible sources of information described above — plus a few extra ones you may want to consider.

Some of the sources are likely to be more useful to you than others, and some may not be available to you in your area. All the same, you should have no great difficulty getting the information you need about open learning packages and support services.

Possible sources

- Catalogues from producers
- *Open Learning Directory*
- Open College/Open University centres
- Other universities
- Other delivery centres (local colleges, etc)
- Local education authority (contact the organizer for adult education)
- Local education guidance centres
- Public libraries (reference section)
- Your employer (contact the personnel or training department to see if they sponsor open learners)
- Your trade union or professional association
- JobCentres
- Training Access Point offices (TAPs)
- Your local Training and Enterprise Council (or, in Scotland, Company) (TEC).

Any others you are aware of?:

Remember, you'd probably be wise to seek information and advice from more than one source.

Which sources will you try first?:

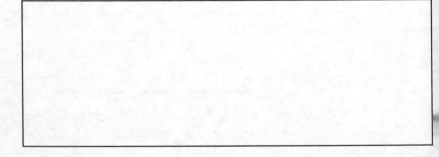

Talking with the providers

Sooner or later, you may want to talk to staff at a delivery centre — either an Open University or Open College centre or one that offers a different range of programmes. What might be your purpose in going to talk with the people who provide open learning? I can see four possibilities. Might any of them be yours? Would you have other purposes as well?

☐ To check that open learning will be right for me.
☐ To discuss where I can learn—e.g. in college, at home, at work, or as I choose.
☐ To find out whether learning packages of the sort I need are available.
☐ To examine materials from the learning packages.
☐ To convince myself that the providers can give me support of the type and quality I need while I am learning.

Others? (What?):

Before your meeting

You may begin weighing up the providers before you even meet them. First impressions may tell you something about the quality of service you are likely to get. For example, ask yourself:

- Was I able to get a reasonable picture — e.g. from printed material or a telephone conversation — of what kinds of services the providers may be able to offer me?

- Was it clear how to make personal contact with the providers?

- Was it easy to make an appointment to see someone?

- In general, do I get the feeling they are both friendly and professional?

Your comments:

When you meet the providers

When you meet the providers, you may like to take along this book and refer to the checklists you tick and any notes you may have made. It's always easier to start this kind of thinking on your own rather than tackle it from scratch in a meeting where time will be limited. This prior thinking should get your discussion off to a good start.

**You
are the
customer**

One important thing to remember in talking with providers is this: you are the customer. You are not begging favours from the providers. You are considering whether you want to buy something from them. Without people like you they cannot stay in business.

With open learning, it's your requirements that are meant to be supreme — not those of the providers. However, you will probably find that the people you speak to will go out of their way to help you. They are usually people with a commitment to education and training as well as to their particular organization. They are not like the hard-nosed sales staff we sometimes run up against in buying used cars or double-glazing. If their organization can't offer something that suits your needs, they are quite likely to suggest another provider who can.

To make the best use of your time with the providers, it is worth thinking about your agenda. What are the main questions you want to ask in the meeting?

The fact that you've got an agenda will show that you have given serious thought to what your needs are. This should make clear not only that you don't intend to waste the providers' time but also that you expect them to treat you seriously and professionally.

**After
your
meeting**

You probably won't sign up for a programme at your first meeting with the providers. You'd be wise to reflect on what you've got out of the meeting before you agree to anything binding.

Here is a checklist to help you do so. You may find it worth looking at **before** the meeting. It may suggest some extra issues you want to raise or points you want to look out for.

Attitudes

☐ Did the person I met make me feel welcome?

☐ Were they prepared to listen to me (rather than giving me a standard talk)?

☐ Did they understand what I want out of learning?

☐ Did they pay attention to my needs and preferences?

Options

☐ Were they able to discuss alternative ways in which my needs might be met?

☐ Did they seem knowledgeable about a range of open learning programmes (packages and support)?

☐ Did they suggest options rather than pushing one particular programme?

☐ Were they able to help me consider the pros and cons of different programmes in the light of my needs and preferences?

☐ If a package was almost but not quite right for my needs, were they able to suggest ways it might be modified to suit?

☐ If they were unable to provide a programme to suit my needs, were they able to suggest other ways I might get myself a suitable programme?

Trying it out

☐ Did they let me look at open learning materials from one or more packages that might suit me?

☐ Did they give me time to read some of the material and think about what it might be like to learn from?

☐ If they suggested computer-based material, did they let me try it out?

☐ If they suggested a package they didn't have available, were they willing to get a copy for me to see?

☐ Were they willing to put me in touch with existing (or recent) learners so that I could ask them how they felt about the programme?

The support service

☐ If we did find a package that might suit my needs, did they make clear what kind of support they could provide me with? — e.g.
~ the type and amount of tutor support
~ support in my workplace (e.g. mentoring)
~ access to equipment
~ access to other learners on the programme
~ help with accreditation/qualifications.

☐ Did they take into account my previous experience of learning and discuss what learning skills I might already have or need help with?

☐ If I wanted some existing experience or learning assessed so as to save me from having to repeat stuff I know already, were they willing to help me in this?

☐ Did they make clear what the open learning programme will cost me? — including
~ package materials
~ additional books or materials
~ use of equipment (if any)
~ cost of support services
~ costs of any tutorials/group meetings/residential sessions, etc
~ assessment/accreditation/qualification costs.

☐ Did they make clear how and when I would pay? e.g. were instalments possible?

☐ Did they have any suggestions as to how I might get help with the costs?

Overall

☐ All in all, do I feel that the providers dealt openly with me rather than trying to sell me one particular line regardless of my needs and preferences?

If the answer to most of your questions is YES, then it looks like the providers are playing fair in helping you decide what best suits your needs.

After each meeting you have with providers, I suggest you review the meeting and fill in the following summary. List the advantages of buying from that provider, the disadvantages, and the uncertainties — where you need more information:

Advantages	Disadvantages	Uncertainties

Perhaps no one provider will be able to satisfy all your requirements. Each will have their different pluses and minuses. Doing this comparison will perhaps help you decide where to compromise.

Clear up your doubts

Before you do so, you will of course want to clear up any uncertainties you may have. For example, will the quality of the providers' support service live up to the quality of their advice service? For instance, will you get sympathetic tutors who are available when you most need help and who comment on your work promptly and helpfully? To be sure about that you may need to speak to learners who've had experience of the programme. Ask them what they feel about the support they've been getting.

Again, you may not yet have seen the package being offered by the provider. If not, you will probably want to read through some of the materials before you decide which provider to buy from. If you like the package, then it will count as an advantage of buying from that provider. If you're not 100% keen on the package and regard it as something of a disadvantage, you may still settle for that provider because they offer you exactly the kind of support you feel you need.

What do you think of the packages?

If the subject you want to learn about is a popular one, you will have a choice of materials. Several different producers may have developed packages — often at different levels or for different types of learner.

Making a choice
So you will want to compare them in order to make your choice. How close is each one to meeting your needs? Do they all appear to be high quality productions? Which one offers best value for money? (This won't necessarily be the cheapest.)

It is impossible to make these decisions just by looking at catalogue descriptions. You need to see the materials themselves. Even when you appear to have no choice — when only one package comes anywhere near to meeting your needs — you will still need to see it before you can be sure it is worth spending time and money on.

How can you get to see the package materials? The producers are unlikely to send you sample copies and even the largest libraries are unlikely to have more than a sprinkling of open learning materials. It is possible you'll know a learner who has just the package you are interested in. But your most likely way of getting to inspect some packages is through your contact with the providers.

What do you want?

So let's suppose you get to see a likely-sounding package. What are the main things you would be looking for in deciding whether it is right for you?

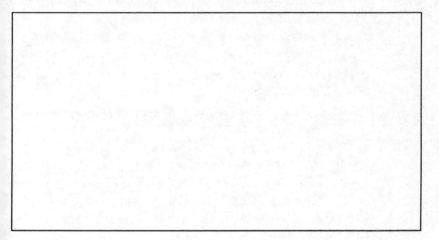

Questions to ask

Have you already read Chapter 4 ("How does open learning work?")? Or have you seen a variety of open learning materials already? If so, you'll probably have a pretty clear idea about what to look for in a package. Whether you have or not, here is a checklist of questions you may want to ask yourself when examining open learning materials. Tick any that you think important:

Coverage

☐ Does the package clearly state what it is meant to do for me — i.e. what I should be able to do as a result of working through it? (Aims and objectives)

☐ How closely do these aims and objectives tie in with my needs and expectations?

☐ If the aims and objectives are not clearly set out, is there any other indication as to what I might learn from it — e.g. does it contain tests or is it aimed at a particular qualification?

☐ Does the package cover more topics or objectives than I really need?

☐ If there are sections of the package I am already familiar with, can I skip them in order to save time — and not be penalized?

Structure

☐ Are the package materials attractive to look at and easy to handle?

☐ Is there a clear explanation of what's in the package and how to use it?

☐ With a computer-based package, are there clear operating instructions?

☐ Does the package suit the ways I like to learn?

☐ If it involves media other than print (e.g. computers or video) shall I be able to get access to the necessary equipment?

☐ Is it divided into manageable chunks of learning?

Teaching style

☐ Is the language clear and user-friendly?

☐ Do the contents seem interesting and relevant?

☐ Are there plenty of helpful examples?

☐ Are all technical terms carefully introduced and explained?

☐ Does the author seem to be generally on the same wavelength as me?

Activities and assessment

☐ Are there frequent "activities" to help me apply the ideas I am learning about?

☐ Do enough of these get me to do something practical rather than simply answering questions?

☐ Is it clear how I will get feedback on such activities — e.g. from author's comments or sample answers?

☐ Are there any self-tests to let me assess whether I have achieved my learning objectives?

☐ Are there any computer-marked tests?

☐ Are there any exercises or assignments for marking by a tutor?

☐ If the package is geared towards some kind of formal assessment, is it of the kind I want — e.g. is it based on written work and/or examinations or on observations of my practical ability to carry out tasks at work?

Reputation

☐ Who were the producers who developed the package materials?

☐ Do they have a good reputation for producing quality materials?

☐ Can I find out (e.g. from the providers) whether this particular package (or similar packages if it is one of a series) has been used already by people like me?

☐ If so, can I find out how helpful it was to them?

Value for money

☐ How much will the package cost me?

☐ Does it seem to offer value for money?

☐ How do I rate it compared with competing packages (if any)?

Remember: it's unlikely that anyone will have produced the perfect package to meet all your individual needs and expectations. The trick is to find one that looks like meeting enough of them to offer reasonable value for the money, time and effort you'll need to put into working with it.

Agreeing your open learning programme

Let's say you've found a reasonably acceptable package. This will form the core of your open learning programme. But the learning programme = package **plus** support. To make up the complete programme, you will need to be sure that the provider will be able to give you the support service you need.

You will now need to go into a certain amount of detail before you agree that programme with the providers (and start handing over your cash). Firstly, you will want to know what demands the package will be making on you. Secondly, you will want to confirm that the providers will be able to give you the support you need.

The package's demands

This first checklist concerns what the programme will be demanding of you. Tick off the items you think worth asking the providers about:

Time

☐ Does the package have a timetable that will make difficulties for me, or can I start at a time that is convenient to me?

☐ Can I spread my work on it over as long a period as I want (or complete my work in a short period if I want to)?

☐ How many hours per week will I need to devote to learning?

☐ For how many weeks?

☐ Can I find this amount of time?

☐ Will I need to take any time off work or give up any holiday?

Skills and equipment needed

☐ Does the package assume that I already have certain knowledge or competence — e.g. knowledge of technical terms or ability to use a computer?

☐ Do I have this knowledge or competence?

☐ What learning skills will I need?

☐ What media will I need to learn from— e.g. books, video, computers, etc?

☐ What equipment will I need to have access to — e.g. computers, vehicle engines?

☐ Will I need to buy or rent any books or equipment in addition to the package itself?

☐ If so, are they easily available and what will they cost?

Travel and workplace

☐ Do I need to travel anywhere?

☐ What classes or other group meetings might I need to attend — where and how often?

☐ Do I need to go somewhere to meet a tutor — if so where and how often?

☐ Does the package expect me to carry out activities in a workplace?

☐ If I need to study or carry out any activities at work, will this be OK with my employer?

☐ If I need to use any of my employer's equipment or facilities, will this be OK?

Assessment

☐ Will I need to show examples of my work for assessment or to demonstrate my practical competence?

☐ Do I have any choice about what will be assessed?

☐ If my work is to be assessed, will there be deadlines I need to meet?

☐ Can such deadlines be stretched if I meet difficulties?

☐ Is there an examination — if so, where and when?

☐ If I am not successful in the exam, how soon can I retake it?

☐ Can I retake it without having to take (and pay for) the whole programme again?

Any more questions you've thought of now you've read the list above?:

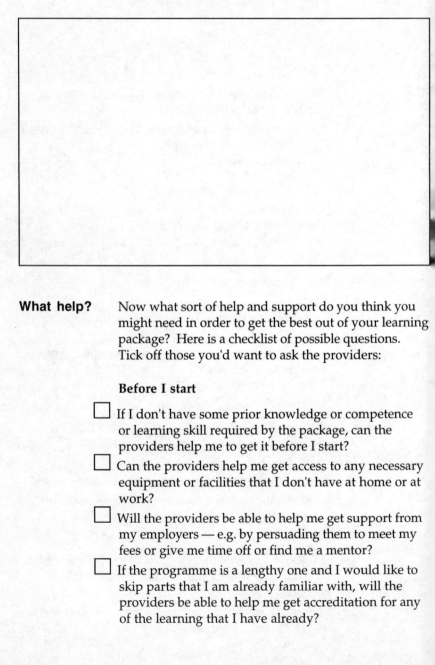

What help?   Now what sort of help and support do you think you might need in order to get the best out of your learning package? Here is a checklist of possible questions. Tick off those you'd want to ask the providers:

Before I start

☐ If I don't have some prior knowledge or competence or learning skill required by the package, can the providers help me to get it before I start?

☐ Can the providers help me get access to any necessary equipment or facilities that I don't have at home or at work?

☐ Will the providers be able to help me get support from my employers — e.g. by persuading them to meet my fees or give me time off or find me a mentor?

☐ If the programme is a lengthy one and I would like to skip parts that I am already familiar with, will the providers be able to help me get accreditation for any of the learning that I have already?

While I am learning

☐ Will a tutor be provided for me?

☐ Shall I be able to contact the tutor if I have a problem I'd like to discuss?

☐ Who else will I be able to contact at the providers — e.g. a counsellor or office staff?

☐ Will I be able to get regular feedback on my progress?

☐ How quickly can I get such feedback?

☐ Can I meet other learners?

When I have finished

☐ Will the providers help me get a final assessment of what I learn from the programme — and any relevant certification or accreditation?

☐ Will the providers be able to advise me about how to build on what I will have learned?

Any other questions you'd want to ask?

Are you now ready to sign up for your open learning programme? If the providers look like giving you value for money (and if you can afford it), you may now be able to reach an agreement. What exactly are they providing?

Get it in writing? Some of the following points may be covered in their leaflets and brochures. If some of them are not, you may want to get your providers to answer them in a letter. You are, after all, entering into a contract with them. You want to be quite clear about what you can expect for your money. Tick the questions you still need to see answered in writing:

☐ What materials am I being provided with?

☐ When do I get them?

☐ What are the start and finish dates of the programme?

☐ What assignments or other projects must I complete by which dates?

☐ Are there any other essential dates — e.g. for residential weekends or examinations?

☐ What arrangements are there for meeting other learners?

☐ Who is my tutor and/or counsellor and/or mentor?

☐ Where, when and how (e.g. letter, phone, visit) can they be contacted?

☐ What services can I expect from them?

☐ Are any other services or facilities being provided?

☐ What are the arrangements for assessment and accreditation?

☐ What are the arrangements for payment?

☐ Whom do I contact in case a major problem or emergency disrupts my work on the programme?

☐ Which member of the provider's staff shall I contact if I have any queries or complaints about the way the support service is operating?

Are there any other points you would like to see mentioned in writing?

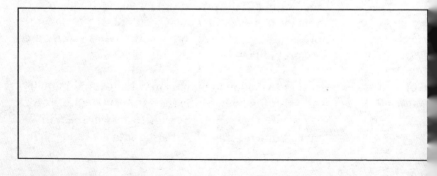

To avoid confusion or ill-feeling later, it is important for both provider and customer (you) to agree what they are expecting of each other right from the start.

If your programme is work-related . . .

You may be doing open learning as part of your training at work. If so, you may want to ask your employer many of the questions we've raised in this chapter. If your employer is using off-the-shelf packages, the producers may be able to provide your organization with a support service. They may be able to provide tutors, for instance, and customize packages so that they better suit the needs of you and your colleagues. If you think you might benefit from such a support service, you may want to ask about it.

What if the open learning programme is not an official part of your training? It may still be worth asking your employer about the possibility of financial or other support. Point out the ways in which it is likely to help you work more effectively and contribute more to the organization. Do this by showing the relevance of the objectives, assignments, projects, etc. of the programme and of any qualifications or accreditation that you expect to get as a result. If nothing else, your employer may agree to pay for the programme if you succeed in it.

If you are unemployed and the package is work-related, you may be entitled to some kind of support from Employment Department funds or from elsewhere. Ask about this at your nearest JobCentre.

If the open learning programme you want to take is one that leads to a "national vocational qualification", you should find that the Inland Revenue is paying for 25% of your course and exam fees. You may want to check with the providers that this has been arranged.

Reflection box

Look back at the objectives at the beginning of this chapter. Do you feel reasonably confident about them? What is the most useful thing you've got from this chapter? How might you apply it?

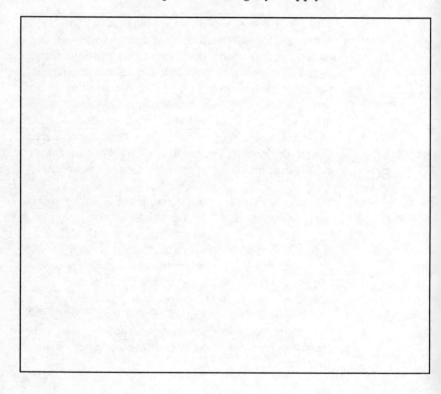

Follow-up activities

1. Send off for catalogues (if you haven't already).
2. Select some likely-sounding packages.
3. Interview a provider.
4. Analyse a package.
5. Sign up for a programme (if you can find one that suits you).

Chapter 6

Getting organized for open learning

---

*With open learning you are mostly on your own.
Even if you have support from a tutor or mentor, they
won't be teaching you — you'll be teaching yourself.
To do this properly, you'll need to get yourself
organized. This chapter tells you what's involved.*

Objectives:

When you've worked through this chapter you should
be better able to:

- Arrange a place or places to study.
- Decide what tools and resources you will need.
- Plan your use of libraries.
- Identify people who might help with your learning.
- Plan your use of time for learning.
- Keep a learning diary.

Organize? Why bother?

Open learning may offer you a new freedom —
perhaps to learn where you like and when you like,
and at whatever pace you choose. But with this
freedom comes a new responsibility. Nobody is
breathing down your neck to make you learn. Your
success will depend on how well you can organize
yourself for learning.

**Possible
problems?**

So what exactly needs organizing? Well, look at the
following list. It shows a number of concerns that
learners have mentioned to me about their efforts to
study. Tick any that might also be true of you:

☐ *"I feel I'm not doing as much work as I should."*

☐ *"One week I'm doing nothing at all, and then the next
I'm suddenly up to my eyeballs."*

☐ *"I often feel too tired to think about studying."*

☐ *"I seem to put things off until a deadline is right on top
of me."*

☐ *"Whatever I'm working on, I'm forever wondering if I
really ought to be studying something else."*

☐ *"I find difficulty getting started; I keep putting it off."*

☐ *"I can't seem to concentrate on study for very long."*

☐ *"I can't find a really satisfactory place to study in."*

☐ *"I'm way behind, and I wonder if I'll ever catch up."*

☐ *"My family think I'm neglecting them because I spend
too much time on studying."*

Any other problems of your own you want to add?:

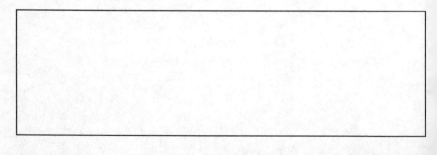

Only you can know how many of the above concerns might be yours. And if they are, how much do they matter? Are any of them serious enough to prevent you achieving what you want to achieve? If so, the rest of this chapter should help you overcome them.

Three needs   There are three things you might need to organize:

- a **place** (or places) in which to study
- the **tools** and resources you'll need to help you and
- the **time** in which to do your studying.

Let's look at these one at a time:

A place to study

Open learners do it in all sorts of places — a bedroom (spare or not), a corner of the dining room table, a converted garden shed, a college library. They even do it on buses, in bars, and on park benches when the weather is kind.

If your open learning is part of your workplace training you may have a place you can study at work. If your course involves computers or other equipment, that may be the only place you can conveniently use it.

Some learners prefer to stick to one study place. That place then becomes so linked with studying that they can slip into the right frame of mind the moment they sit down. Others like to feel there are two or three such places they've got used to studying in. The more the better. Maybe you can use different places for different kinds of studying.

Be prepared   It's best to keep flexible. Don't tell yourself you can't study because you are not in one of your usual places. Be prepared to make good use of unexpected scraps of time in unusual places. Suppose you find yourself stationary for 20 minutes in a tailback on the M6 or are told your dental check-up will be delayed by quarter of an hour. Do you fret and fume? Not on your life. You are organized. You whip out your notebook with some key questions in it, or that photocopied article you've been hoping for a chance to read. And you make the most of time and place.

Home or away?

If you can study undisturbed at home, that may be the ideal place to do most of your studying. You'll have all your package materials to hand, and you may even be able to leave your work out between one session and the next. But maybe home is not a convenient place to work or maybe you enjoy seeing other people around you while you work. So you may prefer to study in a library or some other public building you have access to — e.g. by arriving early or staying on late at work.

What conditions?

Ideally, your study place should have plenty of light and fresh air and be neither too hot nor too cold. You also need a desk or table, and a chair that is comfortable to sit in for longer than you might normally be sitting in a chair. And what about noise? Personally, I am easily distracted by noise, especially the musical variety. But some people (like my dentist) say they can hardly concentrate without it. You may want a place where you can escape from other people's sounds. Or you may want to be able to make your own sounds without disturbing other people.

Can you arrange all these working conditions to your satisfaction at home? Or will you be able to find satisfactory conditions only in some place like a library or community centre — which may be a long bus ride away and not always open when you want to study?

It's almost impossible to get perfect conditions, but one can often improve them. For example, I find that even my central heating system won't keep me warm when I'm sitting still for long periods, as I do when writing a book. That's why, if you could see me now, you'd notice my body and legs are snugly tucked inside a padded sleeping bag. Fortunately, it's a quiet day around the house or you might see me sporting ear-plugs as well.

**Other
people?**

Whether you can study satisfactorily at home may also depend on who else lives there with you and whether they can also live with your studying. If you are under the same roof as family or friends, have you talked about your open learning with them? Do they understand what it requires of you? They may be making demands on you, or doing things of their own, that interfere with your studying. If so, tell them about the effects they are having. Listen to how things seem from their point of view. Try to reach some sort of workable compromise.

What will be your main problem in finding somewhere suitable to study? What might you do to overcome it?

If you are having trouble sorting something out, discuss it with people who might help. Friends, tutors, mentors, employers, a local college, other learners — any of these may have ideas you can build on. I know one open learner who did most of her studying for an Open University course in other people's houses — while acting as a baby-sitter.

Organizing your tools and resources

Let's deal with the obvious things first.

What tools do you need?

Here is a list of "tools", some of which you will find essential, some merely desirable, and some not necessary at all. Tick those that will be essential for work on your open learning programme:

☐ pads of writing paper (lined or unlined, A4-size?)
☐ one or more A4 ring binders
☐ cardboard A4 wallets or folders
☐ a stapler
☐ paper clips
☐ a hole puncher
☐ rings for reinforcing holes
☐ one or more box files to store cuttings, pamphlets, etc.
☐ a box big enough to contain all your course materials
☐ ballpoint pens
☐ coloured and plain lead pencils
☐ a pocket notebook
☐ a diary
☐ a year planner
☐ a pocket calculator
☐ other instruments
☐ a good dictionary
☐ a thesaurus
☐ other reference books
☐ essential books not provided as part of your package
☐ other items (what?).

Perhaps you won't be entirely clear what's essential until you are well into your course. You won't want to waste money buying items you may never use. But some items really will be necessary if you are to work efficiently and produce acceptable results. Don't try to get by without those essential tools.

What resources?

So much for tools. Now what resources are you likely to need? Most of them will no doubt be supplied by the package itself — workbooks, tapes, practical kit, or whatever. With some programmes you may need access to computers, language laboratories, video playback machines, electronic equipment or whatever. If so, that will probably be arranged by the people from whom you are buying your programme. Or at least they should be able to advise you on how to arrange it yourself.

Using libraries

Libraries are a key resource for many open learners. Libraries can give you access to an enormous range of information. Most of this will take the form of print on paper — that is, books, pamphlets, journals, etc. Even if they don't have the book you want they may be able to get it reasonably quickly through the inter-library loan system.

In addition to print material, some libraries have audio and video recordings, drawings and paintings, slides and photographs, microfilm of old newspapers, and so on. They may also operate computer databases you can use. Some big libraries even deliver open learning programmes.

Most importantly, all libraries have professionally qualified staff — the **librarians**. Their purpose in life is to help us get the information we need. They are highly trained in finding things out and we can learn a lot from their methods. Don't think of them as book-minders — think of them as information-gatherers.

Which library?

Even if you regularly borrow books from your local public library, you may be unaware of the range of materials and help available. And it may never have occurred to you to try certain libraries at all. So, to begin with, why not check through the different types of library in the following list and tick off any you might be able to get access to:

☐ your local branch of the public library
☐ the main branch of the public library
☐ a mobile library
☐ a public library in another area
☐ a college or university library
☐ the library of a government department
☐ the library of a local business or voluntary group
☐ the library of a trade union or professional body
☐ the library of a local club or society
☐ other libraries (which?).

This list may have led you to think of certain local libraries you haven't tried before. You may wonder whether you'd be entitled to use them. If there is any doubt, perhaps a letter of introduction from someone like a tutor or employer might open the door for you.

Just as a reminder to yourself, write down the name of one new library that may worth be checking out:

To get the best use out of a library, you need to know:

• What subjects it covers.

• What kinds of material it contains (e.g. just print?).

• How to find out whether it has (or can get) what you need.

• Where abouts in the library you'll find different kinds of material.

• What the borrowing arrangements are.

• How to get information on the above topics as and when you need it.

Finding out   The best way to find out what your library can do for
you is to ask the librarians. Larger public libraries will
have an Information or Enquiries Desk and may even
have a leaflet describing the library's services. But
even in the smallest library you should find someone
who will be happy to help you find your way around
the system.

People as a learning resource

Not all learning is to be found in books and the like.
You can also learn from other people — at home, at
work, or in the community. (I've mentioned librarians
in the previous section.) Such people don't necessarily
have to be older than you, more experienced or better-
qualified than you. They don't even have to be more
knowledgeable than you are about the subject you are
studying. Nor do they need to have any official
connection with your open learning programme.

Like whom?   There are all sorts of people who can aid your learning
— even if all they do is lend a sympathetic ear while
you tell them about what you are doing. Consider the
following. Which of them might you expect to get help
from in your open learning programme?

☐ a tutor

☐ a counsellor

☐ a mentor

☐ my boss

☐ colleagues at work

☐ technicians and other specialists at work

☐ local experts and enthusiasts in the community

☐ people who can help me get access to special facilities

☐ librarians

☐ family and friends

☐ other learners doing my programme

☐ learners who've done it before
☐ learners doing related open learning programmes
☐ others (whom?).

I am sure you'll have ticked several boxes. Most of us have quite a few human resources we can draw on. Using them well may take a bit of organizing. In particular, you need to weigh up each one's special qualities — e.g. what sort of help can you get from other learners that you wouldn't expect to get from a tutor (and vice versa)?

And you may need to think about what you'll give them in return. For example, if you need the support of your family and friends, what can you do to make sure that you keep on satisfying their needs also?

Working with other learners

Other learners can be a particularly valuable resource. Can you can get together with other learners who are doing your open learning programme? If so, you may b able to learn from one another's ideas and approaches besides giving each other moral support when the goin gets tough.

If the programme you're working on is a lengthy one, you may want to get together with other learners to set up a **self-help group**. Such a group may need some organizing at the start. Who are to be the members? When/where/how often/and for how long a session will you meet? How will the agenda for discussion be decided? And so on. But once you've settled into a way of working together, little conscious effort may be needed to keep it running.

Might it be helpful to you on your programme to set up a self-help group with other learners? If so, make a note in the box opposite about how you might get in touch with them.

Perhaps the people running your programme will
arrange for learners to meet one another. If they
haven't offered to, why not suggest it?

That's all I'm going to say in this chapter about getting
help from other people. It can be such an important
part of open learning that I have devoted the whole of
Chapter 8 to it.

Organizing your time

Learners new to open learning are often surprised
about two things — how enjoyable they find it and
how much time it takes. No doubt your life was busy
enough before you started looking at open learning.
So how are you going to squeeze in another
demanding call on your time? The answer is twofold:

1. Plan when you will spend time on study.

2. Make best possible use of the time you do spend.

The first step in planning your time is to decide how
much time you need. How long is the programme
likely to take you overall? For example, an Open
College management course may need 30 hours. But
an Open University computing course may need 400.
Are you planning for a few weeks of study or for
several months?

How much?   To find out how long the course is meant to take, start
by looking at the printed guidance published by the
providers. Look at leaflets about the course,
brochures, study guides, etc. If they don't make it
clear, ask the providers directly.

But the figures quoted by providers are often rough
averages. Perhaps half the learners who take a
particular programme will find they need to spend
longer. You may want to ask your tutor or adviser (if
you have one) — or previous users of the programme
(if you can find any) — whether the official figures are
realistic.

When?   You may also want to check whether you are totally
free to spend your study time when you like. For
instance, if you are doing a 100-hour programme, can
you cram all those 100 hours into as little as two weeks
if you want to? Or must they be spread over a much
longer period? This may depend on whether your
programme involves certain events that must happen
at fixed times — e.g. assignments for marking by a
tutor, class sessions or a residential weekend, or tests
and exams. So you may decide there's no point doing
a crash course of 100 hours in your first available
fortnight if the exam is still 4 months away.

So how does this look for your learning programme?
Jot some figures in the boxes below:

   Over how many weeks/months
will you be studying?

   About how many hours per week
will you need to study?

In which weeks, if any, might you need to find extra study time, e.g. in order to prepare an assignment to be marked by your tutor?

Are there any weeks in which you'll have little or no time for study — e.g. because you'll be moving house, working away from home or having a baby?

Is it worth drawing up a calendar for your weeks or months of study, showing any fixed events or deadlines, together with a reminder as to when your time is going to be under greatest pressure? If so, where is the best place to put it so that it keeps jogging your memory about what is ahead — e.g. on the wall by your desk or on the back of the lavatory door?

Finding time Where will you find the time you need? Think back over your activities during the previous week. Which of them would you have had to cut down on if you'd been trying to find the necessary hours for your open learning? How does this affect how much time you'll find and where you'll find it?

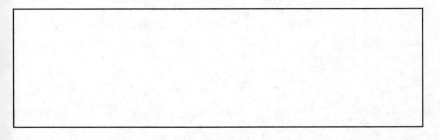

By the way, don't feel that you must find at least one
hour for a study session. Make a habit of using the
odd ten minutes here and the half hour that
unexpectedly becomes free somewhere else. Use them
for those fairly brief study tasks — like rewriting some
scrappy notes or checking what you remember from
your last study session — that are worth doing, but
not in your prime study time.

Also, even if you are allowed time at work for
studying, you may want to invest some of your own
time also. If so, where will you find it?

**Other
people?**

Finally, think about the other people who may be
affected by your programme — spouse, partner,
family and friends. If you are devoting time and
energy to learning will you have less for them? How
are they likely to feel? What might you do to avoid or
overcome bad feelings?

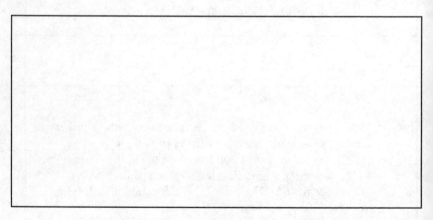

There are no golden rules for keeping things sweet
with the other people in your life. Ideally, though,
you'll try to get them to share your learning goals with
you. How might they benefit from your open
learning? And you will be strict with yourself about
finding time to be with them regularly — and at times
when you are not too worn out to take a proper
interest in their concerns.

Planning week by week

It's helpful to have a long view of what lies ahead of you in your programme. But most learners find they can only plan in a detailed way for one week at a time.

Here are some suggestions as to how you might do it:

1 Draw up a timetable sheet like the one below, showing the seven days of the week divided into morning, afternoon and evening:

	Morning	*Afternoon*	*Evening*
MONDAY			
TUESDAY			
WEDNESDAY			
THURSDAY			
FRIDAY			
SATURDAY			
SUNDAY			

2 Bearing in mind all your regular commitments, mark in all the times when you could study if you chose to do so — e.g. 1 hour on Monday afternoons, 2 hours on Tuesday evening, and so on. You probably won't need all this time, every week; so decide if you want to fix on some of those times as regular study sessions. If so, mark them on your timetable.

3 Fix on a regular time in the week (say Sunday evening) when you can sit down and plan for the coming week.

4 Each Sunday evening (or whenever suits you) check your calender to see if any fixed events are coming up (like an assignment you have to prepare) and decide:

~ what study tasks you want to achieve;

~ how much of your available study time you will need to use; and

~ what you hope to accomplish in each study session.

5 Take your blank timetable and mark in each of your study sessions showing how many minutes you plan to spend in each and what you hope to accomplish. Be as specific as possible here — don't just say "read Unit 3" if you can say "achieve objectives 7 and 8".

6 At the end of each study session:

~ review what you have accomplished;

~ note anything you promised yourself on your timetable in 5 that you've not managed to do;

~ decide how you might need to adjust your future study sessions in order to catch up (or for any other reason); and

~ make any necessary alterations to your timetable

7 At the end of each week (perhaps just before 4 above) reflect on how your actual week has compared with what you timetabled. Don't fret if you haven't kept precisely to your timetable. It may have been too ambitious. Or more important priorities may have cropped up. Just be sure you know **why** you didn't do what you planned to do. What can you learn from the changes you made? Is there anything you need to bear in mind when planning your next week's timetable? (Back again to 4 above.)

Problems?   What is the main problem you see in organizing your time? What might you do to overcome it?

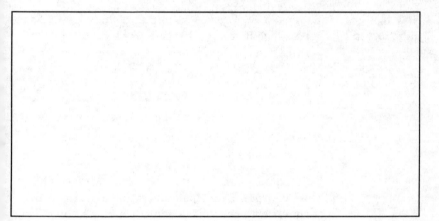

If you do have a problem with finding enough time or with deciding what best to spend it on, some sort of timetabling is well worth trying. I know of many learners who started off feeling this method wouldn't suit them but who ended up well pleased with it. They talk of saving time, getting better results and feeling more confident as a result of their planning and reflection.

Making best use of study sessions

Suppose you are about to sit down to a study session. Whether it's to last 20 minutes or a couple of hours, how are you to get the best out of your time?

The need to prepare   Firstly, you should have given it some thought in advance. If you are trying out the advice I gave about timetabling, you will already have made a note of what study task you plan to tackle. You may have continued thinking about the forthcoming task while walking the dog or coming home from work. Perhaps you'll even have promised yourself that, when you've accomplished what you set out to do, you'll reward yourself with a little treat — like watching that video or going round to visit a friend.

How to get started?

The best way of getting started on a study session is to get started. If you think there's any need to sharpen pencils, make a cup of tea, put the cat out, or make a "quick" telephone call — do it all **before** the time you fixed for the start of your study session. (I speak as an author who can always think of a thousand and one urgent reasons for not getting on with whatever book I'm supposed to be writing.)

Remind yourself of what you want to accomplish. Skim ahead for an overview of the material you'll be working from. Bring to mind any obvious connections with related work you've done earlier. Jot down one or two quick notes or questions. Get stuck in.

How to stick at it?

Once started on your study session, how well can you concentrate? To begin with, you need to know how you work best. For instance, do you prefer to work:

☐ For short periods with long breaks?
☐ For short periods with short breaks?
☐ For long periods with short breaks?
☐ For long periods with long breaks?
☐ For long periods without a break?
☐ Differently according to topic and type of task?

Clearly, there is more than one way of working. People have different concentration spans. You may find that yours varies according to what sort of work you are doing. Sometimes you may become so totally immersed that you lose all track of time — while at other times you are getting up to stretch your legs or make a cup of something every ten minutes or so.

What if you find you've read the same page two or three times and still nothing has registered? Should you try to force yourself to concentrate? Only if it works first time. Otherwise it may make matters worse. You may end up thinking about concentration rather than about the meaning of what you are working on. Better, perhaps, to take a break. Then come back and decide what's gone wrong.

What does it all mean? If you find your are losing concentration, ask yourself about the meaning of what you are working on. Review the work so far. Were there activities in it? If so, did you do them? If you did them, what did you learn? If you didn't do them, do them now. If there weren't any activities, can you think up some of your own? What questions would you ask someone who had read (or written) this material? What objectives does the author say you are working towards? How does the material help you reach them?

If there are difficulties you can't see your way round, make a note of them and go on to something else. Perhaps you'll be able to discuss them on the phone or face-to-face with a tutor. Or maybe you'll be able to get help from a mentor or another learner.

I doubt if you'll be able to concentrate forever, even on something that deeply interests you. You'll need to get up now and again, walk around, stretch, get a drink, focus your eyes on something more distant than the page in front of you. But don't spend so long that you lose the thread of your thoughts.

Getting the habit Some learners find that concentration is a habit they have to acquire bit by bit. If you can't concentrate for an hour at a time, set yourself a goal you can reach in half an hour. If that is too much for you, set yourself 15 minutes' worth of work. Once you know that you can keep busy for a short spell, you should be able to gradually build up your concentration span.

**Review
every
session**

Never finish a study session without reflecting on what you've got out of it: Did you accomplish what you planned? If not, why not? And what do you plan to do about it? Where do you go from here? Is that the end of the topic? Or do you need to do more? If so, what and when?

Your review may take only two or three minutes, but it's the best way of making sure that whatever you got out of the session will remain with you.

What is the main problem you are likely to face in making best use of your study sessions? What might you do to overcome it?

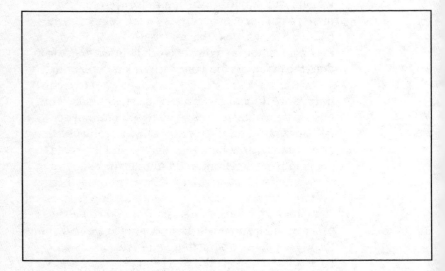

Perhaps the best overall tip for making best use of any study session, however brief, is to be specific about what you want to get out of it. Don't just say: "I'm going to learn a bit more Italian". Say: "I'm going to learn how to use the perfect tense of the five verbs I already know" or "I'm going to complete the audio exercises in Section 6". Set yourself objectives — so you'll know when you've achieved something.

Keep a learning diary

Many experienced open learners recommend keeping an open learning diary. This is a personal record you make of your thoughts and feelings about your programme as you work through it. It doesn't need a book divided off with days and dates. All it needs is a notebook — or maybe a section within a filofax-type binder — in which you **regularly** write comments about your open learning programme.

"Regularly" is the key word, there. There's no need to write in your diary every day. But it wouldn't be much use unless you did so at least once a week — even if all you've got to report some weeks is that you haven't managed to do any studying.

An obvious time to write a note in your diary is when you are reviewing the previous week and planning your next week's work. But you may want to record your thoughts and feelings at other times also. For this reason it's a good idea to do your diary in a notebook that's small enough to carry around with you. You just never know when a useful thought is going to pop into your mind. And, if you're anything like me, they either get written down at once or they get forgotten.

Benefits

There are several benefits you might get from keeping a learning diary. For instance:

- It prompts you to reflect on what (and how) you are learning — and this helps you learn better.

- It gives you a record of how you have progressed. It can be very encouraging to look back at the puzzled or desperate remarks you were making a couple of months ago and realize that all is now crystal clear to you.

- Even a brief note can trigger your memory about material you studied earlier but had half-forgotten or items you planned to follow up later.

Possible contents

What might you put in your learning diary? Just about anything that occurs to you as a result of your learning programme. You may want to mention, for example:

- Parts of the programme that seem especially useful, enjoyable or difficult.

- New ideas or approaches that seem worth trying out at work or elsewhere.

- Your comments on the results of trying things out.

- Questions you want to raise with your tutor or other people.

- Insights you've had into your own preferred ways of learning or your own abilities.

- Comments on what you've learned from marked assignments or practical work.

- How you feel about your progress.

- Your plans for how to make the most of your strengths and overcome your weaknesses.

Suppose you'd been keeping a learning diary while working through this book. (Or while working on your open learning programme if you've already started one.) Jot down an example of the kind of remark you'd have written in it during this last week:

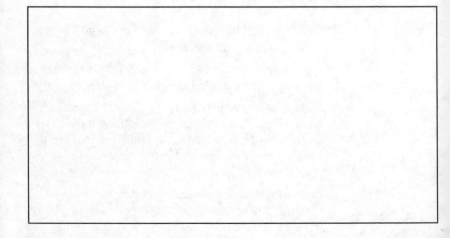

Don't feel you have to write lengthy entries. Two or
three paragraphs a week may well be enough. It
needn't take more than 10-15 minutes — unless you
find it so helpful that you are happy to spend more
time on it.

Reflection box

Look back at the objectives at the beginning of this
chapter. Do you feel reasonably confident about
them? What is the most important thing you've got
from this chapter? How might you apply it?

Follow-up activities

1. If you are worried about time, keep a diary for a week or two. Make a record of how much time you spend on different sorts of activity each day — sleep, work, sport, etc. Consider what changes you might need to make.

2. Visit a library to track down some of the books mentioned in the Booklist at the end of this book. If they don't have the one you want, find out how they can obtain it for you.

3. Consider getting together with other learners to set up a self-help group. (You could begin by discussing some of the ideas in this book.)

4. Start your learning diary (even if you haven't yet started your programme).

Chapter 7

How to tackle your package

What will be in your open learning package? A single workbook? Several workbooks? Plus tapes and other media? Whatever it is, how do you decide where to start and how to get what you need from it?

Objectives:

When you've worked through this chapter you should be better able to:

- Decide how to start work on a package.

- Choose what you will work on and in what order, according to your purposes.

- Use a systematic and effective strategy in learning from workbooks and other package materials.

Getting started

Most people coming to open learning for the first time are a bit anxious about whether they will be able to cope. This is true even for people who have done well at learning in the past. They realize that open learning is different. Nobody is teaching you. You have to do it yourself. You're provided with the materials, but what you make of them is up to you.

Your first problem may be: "How do I get to grips with this great pile of material ?". After all, your package may contain several workbooks, study guides, assignment booklets, audio-tapes and videos, and who knows what else besides. If you imagine that you must somehow get the contents of all that material into your head, then you could feel a little daunted.

What's it all for?

But that's not what it's about, so take heart. Its purpose is to stimulate you — to help you try out new ways of looking at the world and new ways of doing things. You are not expected to memorize it. You are expected to **use** it — to make your own thing of it. And what you make of it will be different from what every other learner makes of it. You may achieve similar objectives to other learners — but the way you apply them will be unique to you.

Dipping in

Perhaps the first step is to check the contents list (if there is one) and see that all is present and correct. But, after that, where do you start work? First, you'll probably want to get the feel of it by just dipping in here and there — wherever your fancy takes you.

You may have seen some of the printed material before you decided to sign up for the programme. All the same, you may want to flip through a few pages of the workbooks or other material. And if you've got an audio-cassette player handy you may want to sample the tapes. Similarly with the video or other materials.

Does it seem user-friendly? Attractively presented?
Relevant examples? Plenty of activities? Do you see
any potential snags or difficulties (like it contains
colour slides and you don't have a slide viewer)?

**Is there
a user's
guide?**

Before you know where you are, you may find yourself
deeply engrossed in the package materials. Hours
may pass before you realize that you've started
half way through a workbook that the authors
intended to be last in the learning sequence. That's all
right. It's your package. You're free to use it as you
like. But if you've found some of the material a bit
puzzling, even gob-smacking, this may be because the
writers expected you to work through certain earlier,
explanatory material first.

So, before you get too carried away, or bogged down,
you might be wise to look for some sort of user's guide.
It may be called User's Guide, Introduction to the
Course, Study Guide, or whatever. It may be printed
as one or more separate booklets or it may be at the
beginning of the first workbook.

**Possible
contents**

Here are some of the things you might find in it.
(When you get your package, or if you've already got
it, you may like to check off the items on this list.)

- Who the package/course is for.
- What the overall aims/objectives are.
- What the package consists of (e.g. workbooks, textbooks, audio-cassettes, etc.).
- An outline of the aims and/or contents of each item in the package.
- Details about any special equipment needed.
- Information about assignments, tutoring, etc.
- Information about assessment, examinations and qualifications.
- Suggestions as to how to work through the package.
- Tips about effective ways of learning from it.

☐ A "map" showing how the various bits of the course connect up.

☐ Information about how the package links up with others you may have studied already or may want to study in the future.

☐ Other information (what?)

Talk about it

So, suppose you've had a browse around the package material and you've read through the user's guide. Without realizing, perhaps, you will already have learned a great deal. You'll probably have a better idea of what the package covers than you did when you signed up for it. You'll perhaps have picked up on some of its main themes or issues. And you'll almost certainly have a better idea of what you can expect to get out of it — and what you might need to put into it (especially if you foresee any problems).

Do you want to share your first impressions with someone? The sooner you get talking about your package, the sooner you'll start making it your own. Write down the name of anyone (more than one if you can) with whom you might discuss it:

Without becoming a bore, talk about your package whenever you can. It's one way of avoiding the loneliness of the long-distance learner — other people's interest can stimulate your own. But it's also a way of learning from other people's views and experiences. Friends, family, fellow learners, tutors, mentors, your boss — they can all take part in your open learning.

Remember your purposes

But other people can't do the work for you. That you must do for yourself. Where do you start? This depends on you, the kind of package you are studying, and what you want to get from it.

Before you start munching your way through that pile of learning materials, pause for a moment. Remind yourself of what you hope to get from the course. Tick any of the following that may be true of you:

☐ A. I want to learn some new skills.

☐ B. I want to learn new ways of looking at the world.

☐ C. I want to be able to say I've completed the course.

☐ D. I want to remember everything in the course.

☐ E. I want to be able to talk intelligently about the course.

☐ F. I want to do well on the assignments/tests/exams.

Others? (If so, note them below.)

How you tackle the course may depend on your purpose. For instance, you may decide you don't need all the package. Or maybe you need to decide your own best route through the materials.

Do you need it all?

Many open learners say that their courses are over-loaded. That is, they contain more material than most learners can work through in the time they have available.

There are several reasons for this. Sometimes the authors have an unrealistic notion about how much time learners are able or willing to spend on the course. Sometimes they just don't realize how much time the material takes to work through. This easily happens when it contains activities that take you out into your workplace or the community.

Sometimes the authors include more material than any one learner can work through — because they expect different learners to chose different **optional** sections within it.

Experienced open learners will look at the time-estimate the providers give for a course and say: "That's an average time. I might need quite a bit longer — maybe half as much again." Not surprisingly, they also say — at the beginning, and from time to time while studying the course — "Do I need all this?"

Suit your purposes

If you agreed with A or B above you may decide to start by flicking through the materials to see which of them cover skills or ideas you are already confident about. You may decide you can miss out sections that cover things you can already do or knowledge you already have. That will leave you free to concentrate on stuff that is new to you.

If you agreed with C or D, you may feel there is no alternative but to work through every bit of material in the course. This may not be so. Students who do well on ordinary courses certainly don't attend all the lectures and read every bit of every book. And they will not remember everything in the course. Nor need you. It's not like in school where, if the teacher taught something, you were supposed to learn it. The course is simply a resource for you to draw on.

You will have satisfactorily completed the course when you have got what **you** need from it — and remembered what is important to you. If that means leaving parts of it untouched, so what? You can always come back to it another time if you ever need it.

Selectivity is a skill

Similarly, with E above. You can talk intelligently about a town you have visited even though you didn't explore every alley-way and speak to every inhabitant. So too with a course. In fact, if you tried to talk about all of it — rather than selecting the bits that made a particular impact on you — then you could end up being a bore. A vital part of learning is being able pick out what is important for **you**.

Finally, what about F above? If you want to do well on assignments and tests, does this mean you have to work through the whole course? Not at all. In fact, many experienced open learners use the assignments — or the test-exercises, if they know what form they will take — to help decide what they can leave out.

Some make this decision at the beginning of their programme. Others may do it later on if they feel time is running out on them. What they say is: "This assignment requires me to do this-and-that with such-and-such information. So which bits of the package material will help me? I'll concentrate on those and maybe come back to the other bits later if I have time."

Do you have any new thoughts about how you might tackle your package?

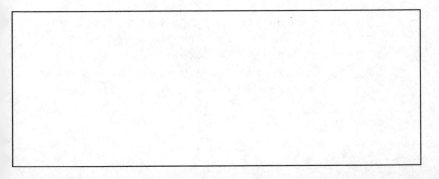

Don't worry if you've decided: "I can't see anything I can safely leave out. I'll try to work through everything". That's perhaps how most open learners begin. You are free to change your mind at any time if that strategy becomes difficult to stick with. You won't be "cheating" if you don't work through it all.

What's your best route?

One more thing before you get started. Do you need to work through the materials in a particular order? Can you start with any section you like — perhaps because it looks most interesting or most useful — and then turn here and there within the package as you please? Or is the package written in such a way that you won't be able to understand parts of it unless you've studied certain other parts first?

For instance, if there's a workbook titled *Advanced Techniques*, then there may be one titled *Basic Techniques* whose content you should have mastered first. Again, if your package contains a textbook or an audio-tape, you may first need to read an introduction to it in a workbook or other printed materials.

The user's guide should help you decide how you can sequence your studies. If it doesn't, you may find clues at the beginning of each part of the course — e.g. in the introduction to a workbook. If you can't find any guidance, it is probably safest to follow the order in which the materials are presented.

Learning from a workbook

There must be many good ways of learning from an open learning workbook. But the one way NOT to tackle a workbook — or any other text — is to start with the first word on Page 1 and just keep reading until you reach the last word on the final page.

A 3-stage strategy

You'll probably get more out of it if you use the following strategy which has three stages:

- Previewing
- Reading carefully
- Reflecting.

Stage 1— Previewing

Always spend a few minutes previewing a book before you think of reading it carefully. Preview it by skim-reading — that is, by turning through the pages and glancing at its main features. The purpose of this is to get a general idea of what it's all about and whether it is worth spending more time on.

Preview the book as a whole before you read carefully any of its sections. Then, when you do come to read a section carefully, skim it again before you do so.

Here are some of the key features you may want to look out for during your preview skim:

Key features:	may tell you:
Introduction or first paragraphs	*What it's about*
Objectives/tests	*What you'll learn to do*
Activities	*What you'll do in order to learn*
Symbols	*Whether you need to use other media*
Headings	*Where each topic begins and ends*
Illustrations	*What the subject looks like*
Summaries	*What the main points are*

NOTE: You'll find more details about such features as these in Chapter 4 if you haven't already.

Are there any other features in the sort of books you'll be working with that may be worth a glance while previewing? If so, what might they tell you?

Whatever you find to look at while you are previewing, it should help you to decide:

- which sections are worth reading carefully
- what you might expect to get out of them
- how relevant they are to your needs
- how you might best tackle them.

In particular, look out for symbols or notes telling you that you are expected to turn aside from the print at some point, perhaps to listen to an audio-cassette or go off and talk with other people. In such cases, you'll want to make sure that your equipment or your people are available for you before you begin that section.

If you didn't preview **this** chapter before you started reading it, I suggest you skim through it now. (Don't forget the objectives on the first page.) Jot down a couple of thoughts that occur to you as a result:

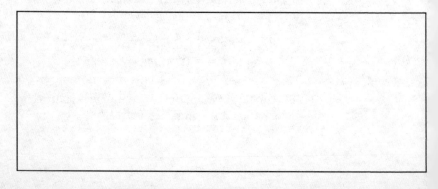

What you get from a preview may be quite different from what another learner would get. You may, for example, have estimated how long the chapter is likely to take you. Or you may have decided that you don't need to read any more of it. Or your preview may have raised questions that you hope a careful reading will help you answer. And so on.

Stage 2—Reading carefully

Now for the second stage of our 3-stage strategy. Having completed your preview, you decide to read a particular section carefully. Here are some suggestions to help with careful reading. Which of them sound right for you?

☐ A. If you come across a bit you can't understand, don't get stuck or give up; just carry on reading the material that follows.

☐ B. Pay attention to all examples and case studies because you may still learn from them even when the situations described are not much like yours.

☐ C. Don't expect to agree with every word in your books; be critical and expect the authors to prove their points to your satisfaction.

☐ D. Think about all the activities but don't feel you must always carry them out in order to learn.

☐ E. Put your own mark on the book — e.g. by underlining or using a highlighting pen, by writing in your responses to activities and by writing comments in the margin.

☐ F. Make notes only if making them helps you to come to grips with the book or if you can see a use for them later; don't make them just because you think you ought to.

Some comments on suggestions A-F above:

Pressing on

On (A) above: We often have to read something two or three times before we understand it. But don't get bogged down. If it still doesn't make sense, skip it and read on. You can always come back to it later — and when you do you may find that what you've read since has helped you overcome the difficulty.

You may want to make a note of anything you don't understand or are not sure about. Perhaps you'll be able to discuss it with a tutor or a colleague later on.

Keep an open mind

On (B): Don't ignore examples about, say, building societies or jazz just because you are more interested in, say, oil refineries or opera. Authors can't always think up an example that will be equally relevant to all readers. But you can learn from examples based on situations you are not too familiar with. Just look for the underlying ideas that the example is trying to put across. Then think up some examples in an area you are more familiar with.

Be critical

On (C): The typical open learning workbook will have been produced with a good deal more care than the typical textbook or training manual. But this doesn't mean it is perfect. The workbooks you read have all been produced by human beings. Human beings don't always agree. A different set of experts would have produced a rather different workbook. And human beings also make mistakes. The experts may have missed something. Or the piloting may not have shown up the difficulty that now faces you. So don't treat open learning materials as holy writ. If you disagree with something in the text it's just possible that your viewpoint is as good as (if not better than) the author's.

Activities

On (D): Activities are sometimes labelled "self-assessment questions" or "in-text questions"— and sometimes they aren't labelled at all. Their purpose is usually to help you understand the ideas in the text or to apply them to your own situation or to analyse and record your own experience or attitudes. Perhaps you won't always need that help. Sometimes the author's comments or "feedback" after the activity will give you all the guidance you need. So you may be able to skip some activities. That's for you to decide.

Sometimes you'll find you won't learn much unless you do complete certain activities. Perhaps they will be the only way of achieving certain objectives you are trying for. Be careful not to skip the ones that really matter for you. Does the user's guide or introduction to the package give you any guidance about activities? Some authors will add a note to certain activities telling you which of the learning objectives each is meant to help you with.

Some authors will suggest how much time you might spend on the activity — e.g. five minutes or half an hour. You needn't follow this advice to the minute, but beware of spending very much longer than suggested unless you think you are getting even more out of the activity than the author expected you would.

Making your mark

On (E): Many people are a bit nervous about writing or drawing on the pages of a printed book. Clearly, you won't do this if the book doesn't belong to you. But, if your open learning materials are your property, you should feel free to mark them up to suit yourself. They will probably have been designed in such a way that you are expected to write in your responses to activities. Some leave so much space for this that one open learner I know said: "They're expecting me to write more of the book than they wrote themselves."

Apart from writing in the answer spaces, you may want to make your mark elsewhere on the pages. You may want to underline important bits — or mark them with a coloured highlighting pen. You may want to write comments in the margins or put a big question mark alongside something you don't understand and want to check up on later. You may want to note your objections to something you disagree with.

All this is perfectly all right. Regard the book as a tool. Make it your own. Customize it to suit your purposes. This is exactly what the authors will be expecting you to do.

**Notes
as well?**

On (F): So you'll probably be writing quite a bit on the pages of your workbooks. Do you need to write separate notes as well? Maybe, or maybe not — or not often. Only do it if you find it useful at the time or if you believe the notes will be useful to you later — perhaps to jog your memory. In any case, you may prefer not to make notes while you are actually reading. You may prefer to save this for the next stage — while reflecting on what you have read.

Now for the final stage of our 3-stage strategy for tackling a workbook:

**Stage 3—
Reflecting**

It's usually not enough just to preview a text and read it carefully — even very carefully. You also need to reflect on it. There are a number of questions you might ask yourself at this stage. For instance:

• How much do I remember about what I've read?

• What were the author's main points?

• Which of them were new to me?

• Do I understand them all?

• Do I want to follow up on any of them?

• Which can I apply in my own life or work?

• How did I get on with the activities?

• Which of the objectives have I attained?

• Has the author answered any questions I had about the topic?

• Has the material raised questions that I hope to see answered in the pages that follow?

• Is it worth my making some notes?

This process may take a few seconds or several minutes. It depends on how much you've read since you last reflected — and on how much of value you've found in the material so far. You may want to glance at parts of the text again during this stage — perhaps to check your recall of the main ideas or to pick up details you want to add to your notes.

Think of the workbooks and other texts you'll be reading. How often do you think you should pause to reflect in this way? For example, after every...

☐ sentence?
☐ paragraph?
☐ section?
☐ chapter?

There are no rules about how often to reflect. However, you probably won't need to stop after every sentence unless the sentences are long and complex. You'll normally need to read at least a paragraph to see what the author is getting at.

You may want to reflect very briefly at the end of some paragraphs. You'd perhaps be even more likely to stop and reflect at the end of a section — perhaps each time a new heading comes up. And you'll surely need to pause at the end of a chapter and think about what you've read and what you've learned from it.

Try it out
This might be a good time to reflect on what you have read in this chapter so far. Try it now and jot down your thoughts in the box below:

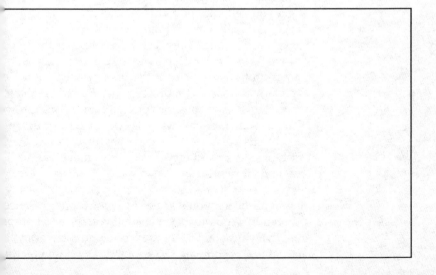

Learning from non-print media

Most open learners do most of their learning from books. That's why I've said so much about reading. But you may have to use media that don't rely on print — for example, audio-cassettes, videos, practical work, computers. What sort of strategy do you need for learning from non-print media?

3 stages

Some of the same ideas still apply. In particular:

1 Preview the work if you can. Maybe there'll be printed notes that will tell you what to expect or maybe you can ask a tutor or a learner who's already been through it.

2 Do the work carefully (if you've decided it's worth doing at all). How many of the six points we discussed under "Reading carefully" can you apply to your work with other media?

3 Reflect on what you've covered, what it means to you and what you've got out of it. Since other media aren't so easy to refer back to as print, you may want to make a note of the main points.

Audio & video

If you are trying to learn from audio or video material — whether broadcast or on tapes — the main thing is to get yourself into the right frame of mind. Most people normally have the radio on only for background music. They rarely give it close attention — except for the occasional news item. People perhaps follow television rather more closely — especially if it's a sports programme. But most look to their television screens for entertainment. They are likely to watch (or half-watch it) with their feet up and their brains in neutral. They are happy just to let it wash over them and they don't expect much of it to stay in their minds.

But, as a learner, you will need to approach it differently. You must expect what you see and hear to alter the ways you look at the world and the ways you act. So you need to take it seriously. How can you do this? Mainly you need to use the same strategy as with other learning — preview, do, reflect.

Some producers of open learning packages will provide printed notes to back up their audio and video presentations. You may need to refer to these before and after (and maybe even during) the presentation. This will help you get maximum benefit from it.

In addition, try to get as much control over the medium as you can. If it is a radio or broadcast programme, record it if possible. Then you will be able to watch it and re-watch it at times to suit you. You will also be able to stop and start it and play any puzzling bits over and over until you understand them.

Most open learning providers give you cassettes anyway, these days, rather than broadcasting the material. If so, they may well build in activities that require you to stop the tape every so often and do something. So, if you know it's going to be that sort of tape, don't plan to listen to it while doing the ironing or driving a car. Save it for a time when you can sit down with it as you would a workbook.

Group work
Some tapes — especially video-tapes — you may get to see only in the company of other learners. Viewing as one of a group you will lose the benefit of being able to control the presentation. You probably won't be able to stop and start the tape or rewind and replay it. But you will have the **extra** benefit of being able to discuss it with other people and hear their points of view. If a tutor is leading the group, you may get yet another useful angle.

Even if you must use cassettes on your own, you may often find it useful to get someone else — not necessarily a fellow learner — to sit through some of the material with you — or at least let you tell them about it afterwards.

Will you be using audio or video material in your open learning programme? If so, who might you usefully get to share it with you?

Practical work

Practical work is a feature of some open learning programmes. Like many other parts of your programme, you may be able to leave out the practical work if you don't want to do it. But if your course includes practical work, then the authors will have included it for a purpose. It will be meant to help you practise certain skills and attain certain objectives.

Suppose you are learning some practical competence — like how to weld or cook or interview people. You clearly won't learn these skills just by reading about them — or even by watching videos of other people practising them. You will need to practise the skills yourself — and get some feedback. You may find it's more difficult than it looks — or easier — or just different.

If you think you've already attained the skill or objectives being tackled by a particular bit of practical work, then perhaps you don't need it. If you can already cook a chocolate sponge cake then you may not see the need to practise cooking a lemon sponge.

But be careful. The competence being taught by the practical work may be different from the one you've got already and you could miss something important. You may also find that doing the practical work helps bring to life the rest of your open learning package.

Suppose you are learning, say, about the psychology of retail selling. Then a morning spent observing and making notes about shoppers' behaviour in a supermarket may bring to life the material you are reading and help you see the truth of it.

Other media?   Might you be learning from other media besides print in your package? (Apart from audio and video and practical work, you may be using computers or other media I haven't mentioned.) If so, could you still tackle them with our 3-stage strategy? How would you apply it?

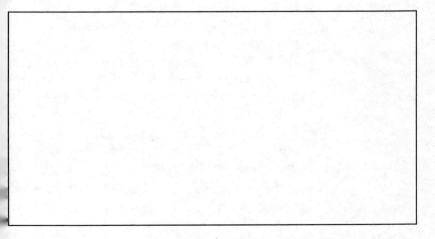

You may well have decided that you should be able to get a lot of benefit from the 3-stage strategy no matter what medium you're learning from. That is:

1. Preview — either by reading printed notes or by asking people about it — to find out what it will involve, what you are meant to get out of it, and whether you need to do it.

2. Carry it out — following any of the guidelines for careful reading that seem appropriate to this non-print reading.

3. Reflect afterwards on what you have learned from it and what you might need to do as a result — e.g. practise some more, make a note of your experience, talk to people about it, re-read parts of the package.

You should even be able to apply it in learning from tutors and other learners (see Chapter 8).

Combine learning with living

Perhaps the wisest overall strategy for an open learner is this: Aim to combine your learning with your living. For example:

- Day by day, ask yourself what you have learned from the day's events — whether about things, ideas, other people, or yourself.

- Always carry a notebook so that you can jot down those thoughts or questions that occur to you at unexpected times and might otherwise get forgotten.

- If you are doing a course, always carry in your mind some problem or issue you can turn your attention to if you get an idle moment.

- If you are learning practical skills, see what you can learn by watching or working with people who are good at them.

- Make a habit of chatting with other people — friends, family, colleagues — about what you are learning.

- Remember that there is no one best way of being an open learner. Consider all the advice you get and pick up what seems useful from the way other learners learn — but concentrate on finding out the strategy that is best for **you**.

What other ideas occur to you for combining your learning with your living? Make a note of them in the box below:

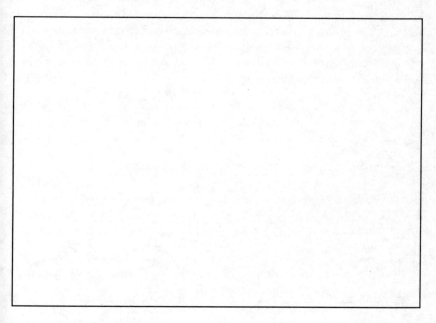

Reflection box

Look back at the objectives at the beginning of this chapter. Do you feel reasonably confident about them? What is the most important thing you've learned from this chapter? How might you apply it? (Make your notes in the box overleaf.)

Follow-up activities

1. Try applying our 3-stage strategy for tackling an open learning workbook. If you've got a workbook you've been waiting to start on, try it on that. Otherwise, apply the approach to any chapter in this book that you haven't read yet. Make a note of how it works for you.

2. When you get your package, remind yourself of the ideas in this chapter and see which of them you find helpful in getting to grips with your materials.

3. Make a note in your learning diary (see Chapter 6) about approaches that work for you.

4. If you haven't yet read Chapter 4 ("How does open learning work?"), you might find it useful to do so before you tackle a package.

Chapter 8

How to get help from other people

Open learning depends on packages. But the package is rarely enough. Open learners need support from other people. In this chapter we explore the kinds of help you may need and how best to get it.

Objectives:

When you've worked through this chapter you should be better able to:

- Anticipate the kinds of problem or difficulty you may have as an open learner.

- Recognize those you may be able to get help with.

- Outline the kinds of help you might like from tutors, counsellors and mentors.

- Identify other people who may give you help informally.

- Make the most of the help available.

Why might you need help?

Being an open learner can be very rewarding and even enjoyable. You may be amazed at how well you can learn on your own and how confident you feel as a result. Open learners will often tell you how it has transformed their lives — especially if they have unhappy memories of earlier attempts at learning.

But few open learners say it is easy. Not many can survive on packages alone. They need help and support from other human beings.

The fact is, you can run into all sorts of anxieties, problems and difficulties when learning under your own steam. For instance, my big worry when trying to learn a language from a packaged course was whether my pronunciation was really as much like the taped voices as I hoped it was. I needed feedback from an expert.

Potential problems

There are many potential problems and difficulties. Here some suggested by other learners. Tick any of the following remarks that you can imagine making about your own open learning — and/or add any other problems of your own you can foresee:

- ☐ *"Will this programme really be of practical use to me?"*
- ☐ *"I'm having trouble finding the time."*
- ☐ *"I'm not sure I know enough about how to study."*
- ☐ *"My mates think I'm getting above myself."*
- ☐ *"I was never any use at school."*
- ☐ *"It's costing me an arm and a leg."*
- ☐ *"Some parts of the course seem beyond me."*
- ☐ *"Am I really making the progress I should be?"*
- ☐ *"I'm not getting a chance to apply it at work."*
- ☐ *"What if I fail?"*

Any problems of your own?:

You may be lucky enough not to run into any problems. But if you do, and if you are anything like most open learners, they are likely to revolve around the value of what you are doing, the effect it is having on other people and how successful you are going to be at it.

Such problems may simply cause you minor or occasional anxiety — but some may seem so crushing that you think about dropping out. Open learning's open door can become a revolving door that deposits you back on the pavement — if you don't seek help before a problem gets too much to cope with.

Who can help?

Happily, open learning (and even distance learning) does not have to mean solitary learning. You should be able to get help and support from at least one of the following:

- an adviser/counsellor
- a tutor
- a mentor
- your boss
- other learners
- friends, colleagues, etc.

What sort of help?

Between them, your supporters may be able to offer many kinds of help. Some of them are listed below. Which of them might you be interested in?

I might like help and support with:

Before I begin:

☐ working out just what I want from learning

☐ deciding the best way of achieving it

☐ assessing my present experience and abilities

☐ selecting an appropriate open learning package

☐ finding other learners who have worked through it

☐ deciding what support I might need

☐ obtaining financial help.

Anything else? (What?):

To do with tackling the work:

☐ planning a timetable

☐ getting myself organized

☐ study skills (e.g. reading, note-making, writing, number-work)

☐ learning from new media (e.g. computers)

☐ how to learn in class sessions

☐ learning from other people informally

☐ producing assignments to be marked by a tutor

☐ taking tests and examinations.

Anything else? (What?):

To do with the content of the programme:

☐ how to make sense of it

☐ sorting out misunderstandings

☐ getting an alternative viewpoint

☐ how to relate the content to my own experience

☐ knowing which bits to concentrate on and which I can leave out.

Anything else? (What?):

To do with my job:

☐ seeing how what I am learning relates to my job

☐ getting financial or other support from my employers

☐ getting to use facilities at work

☐ setting up work projects that let me practice what I am learning

☐ having my competence assessed in my workplace

☐ getting my employers to recognize my new competence.

Anything else? (What?)

To do with assessment:

☐ understanding how I am to be assessed and by what standards

☐ getting expert comment on how well I am progressing

☐ learning to assess my own progress realistically

☐ deciding when I am ready to take the final test or exam

☐ psyching myself up for the final test or exam

☐ deciding what to do next when I find out how well I have done.

Anything else? (What?):

To do with me:

☐ getting a realistic idea of my own ability and prospects

☐ keeping things in proportion

☐ coping with stress

☐ getting some fun out of the learning

☐ sorting out conflicts (e.g. between domestic pressures and the programme)

☐ keeping going when I begin to wonder whether the sacrifices are worthwhile.

Anything else? (What?):

Unless you've already started your open learning, you may have ticked only a few of the boxes above. Perhaps you feel that you won't know what sort of help you're likely to need until you're in the thick of it.

That's all right. Just remember this list and come back to it again once you're into your programme. It will remind you of the kinds of help that open learners are most likely to ask for. Fortunately, most learners don't need every kind I've listed.

Get to know your tutor

If you enrol in an open learning **programme**, you will probably be provided with a tutor. Thus, for example, if you enrol for an Open University degree course or for open and flexible learning programmes through the National Extension College or through local colleges or other "delivery agents", you will be buying the services of a tutor. The tutor is a professional whose job it is to help you learn.

Some programmes will also provide you with someone called an "adviser" or a "counsellor". That person's job may be to help you with anything except the course content. For example, you may want to ask her or his advice on how to get financial help or access to special facilities, or on how to get accreditation.

However, if you simply buy a **package** from one of the many producers, it will be left to you to find other people to get help from. One such person might be a "mentor" — for example, a friend or colleague who might be able to help you informally.

If you are doing an open learning course as part of your training at work, your employer may fix you up with someone who acts as your tutor (or mentor). This might be a training officer or a more experienced colleague — or it could be someone from outside your organization. If your employer is using off-the-shelf packages, the providers or some local college may be able to provide tutor support. If you feel this is necessary, ask about it.

So let's assume you will have a tutor. Then the more you know about one another, the better you'll be able to work together. They will want to know about you — in order to make sure they give you the right kind of help. And you'll want to know about them — so as to see them as a human being, not a cog in a vast system.

Who are they?

Suppose, for instance, that you are about to start a new programme and you've been told that you'll get a tutor. Make a list of the kinds of thing you'd like to know about that person:

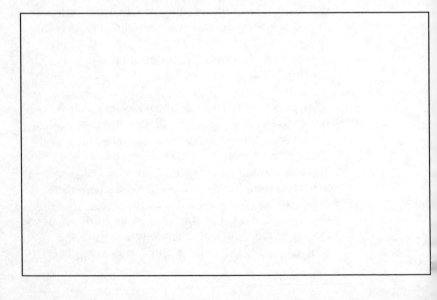

**What's
to know?**

Here are some of the things that other open learners
have said they need or like to know about their tutors:

- name (including first name)
- address
- telephone number(s)
- their availability for telephone calls
- their availability for one-to-one meetings
- their plans for group meetings
- their qualifications
- their experience in the subject of your programme
- any special interests or expertise within the subject
- their previous experience of tutoring the
  programme and/or learners like you
- their other jobs if they are not full-time tutors
- their hobbies, sports, interests other than the
  programme
- family or other personal details.

**Getting
to know**

How will you get such information? Well, if you're
meeting your tutor face-to-face, you may get most of
it in the course of the discussion. Otherwise, your
tutor may send you a letter or a personal biography.

If your tutor doesn't offer you the information you'd
like, then you may want to ask for it. One way might
be to write your tutor a letter, giving information you
think they might like about you, and saying what you
would like to know about them. Few tutors would be
able to resist such a friendly invitation.

You'll probably find you have quite a bit in common
with your tutor. Maybe your children are much the
same age. Maybe you've worked in similar
organizations. Maybe you are both keen on snooker
or rugmaking. But even if you find you are quite
different in most respects, you'll still have one thing in

common — an interest in getting you successfully
through your open learning programme.

**Why do
they do it?**

One thing you might want to know about your tutor is
why she or he does it. You can be pretty sure it won't
be for the money. People with their expertise could be
doing many other things that would pay far better. So
what do you think they get out of it? Why might you
do it, one day, if you are invited to help other learners?

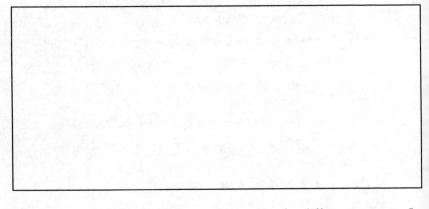

Clearly, different tutors tutor for different reasons. I
asked a group why they did it. Here are some of the
things they said:

- *"I spend most of my work-time managing now, rather
  than practising my specialism — so tutoring other
  people in it keeps me up to date."*

- *"As you know, I'm a lecturer — but that doesn't give
  me the satisfaction of working closely with individuals.
  That's what I get from tutoring."*

- *"I'm very enthusiastic about my subject, so I enjoy
  helping other people to get enthusiastic too."*

- *"I've not been able to teach full-time since I had my
  two small children; so part-time distance tutoring
  means I'm not letting my skills get rusty."*

- *"It's a good incentive for me to extend my own learning
  because every course I've tutored has had some
  elements that have been new to me."*

- *"I find school-teaching very wearying; but tutoring gives me a real lift — dealing with adult learners on first name terms and no discipline problems to worry about."*

- *"I've been an open learner myself and I believe in it; so I want to help others learn the same way."*

- *"Working with mature students who are serious about learning and who produce such high quality work gives me enormous satisfaction."*

Tutor differences

Another thing you may want to know about your tutor is this: Does she or he disagree with any of the ideas in the package? Don't be surprised if this happens. Your tutor may have different experience of the subject or may prefer to approach it differently.

This may not matter. Indeed it may be a good thing and can help you be critical yourself. Who is right: the tutor or the package author? Or are both right in their different ways? But it can be confusing if you don't realize such disagreements are possible, and sometimes common, among experts in your subject.

And what if your tutor is also marking your assignments and they will count towards your overall assessment? Then you may need to explore how safe you'd be in disagreeing with your tutor's line. You may not want to be marked down for your loyalty to the package. And can you trust your tutor to play fair with you if you argue a line of your own?

Extra tutors

If you are on a long or specialized programme you may have more than one tutor. For example, as well as your regular tutor, you may meet someone else for a residential weekend. Or someone else may mark some of your assignments or projects. You probably won't know as much about them as you do about your regular tutor. Just remember that they may have rather different ideas and work in rather different ways. Be prepared to alter your approach.

Agreeing your expectations

One of the first things you'll need to sort out with your tutor is what you expect from one another. Remember that your relationship will probably be different from those you have had with teachers in the past.

This time you are a paying customer. And it is the tutor's duty to provide the services you have paid for. These may be spelled out broadly in the paperwork for your programme. But you may need to agree the details in a friendly discussion with your tutor.

For instance, the paperwork may set certain cut-off dates by which you must get assignments to your tutor for marking. But a chat with your tutor may reveal that she or he may be willing to give you a few days' grace if you really need it.

A learning contract? At the same time, your tutor may ask you to talk through your intentions and set some sort of targets for yourself. Putting what you agree to do along with what the tutor agrees to do can be seen as an informal agreement. Some people in the open learning business might call this a "learning contract". If so, it is rather a fluid one that is liable to develop further as you and your tutor get to know each other better.

Learning from your tutor's comments

For many open learners their relationship with their tutor comes out most clearly when the tutor has to comment on their work — their assignments or projects or practical competence. Many learners may think of this as a form of criticism. So it is, but do remember that criticism involves commenting on the **strengths** of your work as well as on the weaknesses.

How do you feel about the thought of your efforts being commented on?

Many people feel uncomfortable about having their work commented on. It can stir up all kinds of mixed feelings they have about parents, teachers and authority and being dependent on other people's good opinions. It is easy to feel that we personally are being found wanting — not just some aspects of our work. To avoid this calls for sensitivity from the critic and for a relationship of trust between us. We need to feel that the person genuinely has our best interests at heart and is not blaming us or trying to put us down.

What do comments tell us?

Yet learning how to reflect constructively on people's criticism is one of the most useful things we can learn. The only way we can ever grow in competence or understanding is by facing up to our weaknesses and doing something about them. Since we can't always see them for ourselves, it often falls to someone else to point them out to us. That is the purpose of a tutor's comments and suggestions.

In other words, you won't be learning just from workbooks and other pre-packaged materials. You will also learn from your tutor's marks and comments. The marks and comments aren't there just to tell you how well you've done. They're meant to help you do even better. They are part of the teaching.

What do you expect?

Suppose you've finished your first assignment and you've sent it off to your tutor. What will you want from your tutor when she or he returns it to you?

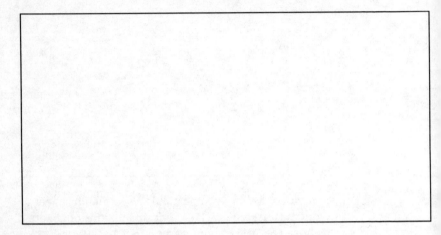

Here is what some other open learners have told me:

- *"I want some reassurance that I'm more or less on the right lines."*

- *"I simply want to know which bits I've done well and which bits I still need to work on."*

- *"I'm happy to have my weaknesses pointed out so long as he gives me practical advice on how to overcome them."*

- *"What I don't want is just a mark. I'd rather get C-minus and lots of criticisms and suggestions than B-plus and no comments."*

- *"I don't mind what she says so long as she gets it back to me before I've forgotten what the assignment was all about!"*

- *"The main thing I'm hoping for is that I can decipher what he's written."*

- *"I want to feel the mark was fair, and that he's understood what I've been trying to do. Where he points out my shortcomings I can usually see what he's getting at."*

- *"I can stand criticisms, but not too many of them all at once. About three things to improve on is the most I can stand being told about."*

- *"I'd like a bit more feedback than I usually get when I've done a particularly good piece of work — not praise, so much as ideas about other good ways of tackling it."*

- *"I like it when they give you plenty to think about; mine's very thought-provoking — she writes almost as much as I do!"*

Providers like the Open University and Open College put a lot of effort into training their tutors. They produce guidelines and handbooks and also run frequent workshops to help their tutors provide the kind of service that learners expect. So the tutors should know what kind of feedback you will expect.

Using the comments

When you get comments from a tutor, there may be a temptation just to look at the overall mark or grade. And feel chuffed or insulted according to how it compares with what you expected. But the most useful thing you can do is reflect on the tutor's comments and suggestions — and learn from them. Here are some suggestions about how to do this:

- Study the comments as coolly as possible to decide exactly what points your tutor is making about your strengths and weaknesses.

- Re-read your assignment — or think back through your practical work — in the light of the comments.

- Decide what improvements you might make (a) in the present assignment and (b) in future work. You may decide it's worth trying to make some improvements in the present assignment — even though they won't be assessed — because it will be good practice for the future. Also you might want to use that assignment later on when revising for an examination.

- If your tutor's advice is not specific enough for you to put into practice, ask for more details.

- Re-read any sections of the package materials that your tutor draws your attention to.

- Re-work a section of the assignment to take account of the tutor's advice.

- If possible, show your rewritten material to your tutor or mentor or to a fellow learner.

- Check through any notes you may have made (e.g. from package materials or class sessions) on the subject covered in your assignment. Be sure they don't echo any of the weaknesses detected by your tutor in your assignment.

- Do any of your tutor's comments suggest you have weaknesses that may run on from one piece of work to another? For example, you may have a habit of presenting opinions without backing them up with proper evidence or of simply failing to read the instructions carefully enough. If so, make a list of such weaknesses. Keep it by you (adding to it if necessary) throughout your learning programme. You may want to use it as a checklist to self-assess each new assignment or project you tackle.

- Read through the comments on your marked assignments again from time to time. It could give you a pleasant sense of progress to see how far you have come since the beginning of your programme.

Quality of comments? Clearly, a lot of your learning could depend on the quality of the comments you get from your tutor. From time to time I meet open learners who are unhappy about the comments they're getting. They say the comments are too few or too vague, or the tutors tell them they have weaknesses but without pointing out examples or suggesting how to improve.

What would you do if your tutor's comments gave you
no clear idea as to how you were doing or how you
might improve your work?

If you feel the comments you are getting aren't
sufficiently helpful, let your tutor know what you
would like — for example:

~ *"You've said I sometimes don't make my points
   precisely enough. Can you point out some
   examples of where this happens?"* or

~ *"Can you suggest a couple of things I might do to
   improve on my . . . ?"* or

~ *"I still don't understand why you say I've misread the
   text. Can you say some more about that?"*

Even the best of tutors will sometimes need to be told
exactly what you would like from them.

**Talking with
your tutor**

How will you keep in touch with your tutor? Maybe
you'll just be sending one another stuff through the
mail. By the way, some tutors and learners have
found it helpful to talk their thoughts into a tape-
recorder and send one another cassettes.

Maybe you'll be able to meet your tutor occasionally.
And perhaps you will have an arrangement for
telephoning one another. If you do phone or arrange
to meet your tutor — e.g. to get help with a learning
problem or explain to them just what you'd like them
to do for you — you may find it worth jotting down a
list of the points you want to raise. Indeed, you may
want to send a written note to your tutor — either

before (in order to get them thinking) or afterwards (as a record of what you've agreed).

Don't be shy about telephoning your tutor if that service is part of your contract. I've spoken to many tutors and counsellors who are sorry that learners don't phone them as much as they should. Too often they tell me that one of their learners has got into a mess or even dropped out and say: "If only he'd called me we could have sorted something out". If you have any problems at all, do make use of that help-line.

Could you use a mentor?

Whether or not you have a tutor, you may also be able to find a mentor. A mentor is someone who takes on the role of helping you learn. How are they different from a tutor? For one thing, your mentor probably won't be paid for helping you. For another, it will probably be someone you choose for yourself.

What they may do

Your mentor could be a friend, someone in your family or someone at work. It should be someone willing to do one or more of the following:

☐ share with you their skills and expertise

☐ help you clarify what you are trying to do

☐ comment on your work when you invite them to

☐ give you emotional support

☐ be an ally and a friend

☐ let you try out your half-formed ideas on them

☐ help you talk through any learning problems you may have

☐ let you know what other people think about you

☐ look out for your interests elsewhere in your organization or community.

Have you ever had help from such a mentor — either at home, at work or in the community? Tick off any of those kinds of help that she or he gave you.

What was it about your mentor that enabled them to help you ? Here are some of the qualities that learners have noticed in successful mentors. (Not all of them in any one mentor, needless to say!) Which of these were true of any mentor who has helped you in the past?

- ☐ a person other people respect
- ☐ good at what they do
- ☐ happy to share their expertise
- ☐ well-disposed towards you
- ☐ generous with their time
- ☐ a good listener
- ☐ willing to accept you for what you are
- ☐ happy to help you become what you want to be
- ☐ able to help you clarify what you really want
- ☐ honest when you ask for their responses
- ☐ constructive in their comments
- ☐ likely to keep your spirits up
- ☐ able to keep your business confidential.

Choosing your own
Can you think of someone with qualities like those who may be able to help you with your open learning programme? Make a note of one or more names:

If your open learning is related to your job, can you find a mentor within your organization? Your line manager may seem like too much of an authority-figure to act as a friendly mentor. Maybe you will want to look to a senior colleague or even to a manager or specialist in another section?

Many organizations are now so struck by the benefits of mentoring that they have set up formal schemes. In others, mentoring is quite common but happens informally. Usually the best mentor will be one you find for yourself. But it is possible to get a good thing going with one who has been chosen for you — provided it's not a task they've just been lumbered with. And besides, is there anything to stop you finding an additional mentor of your own choice?

What's the "contract"?

The mentor role may be informal, but it's still worth making sure that both you and your mentor have the same understanding of what the relationship is. At the very least you may want to agree how often you will meet and for how long, e.g. one hour per week, half an hour per fortnight? And what sorts of help does your mentor think you are looking for?

Can your boss help?

If your open learning relates to your job, you may be able to get help from your line manager. In some open learning schemes, your boss may even be your tutor or your mentor. Whether this suits you will depend, of course, on how you and your boss get on.

Whether or not your boss has a formal role in your programme, might she or he be worth approaching for help with any of the following?:

- ☐ planning my learning programme
- ☐ agreeing deadlines and targets
- ☐ allowing time for me to study at work
- ☐ getting me access to equipment and facilities
- ☐ getting me financial support
- ☐ relating what I am learning to the job
- ☐ helping me practise what I am learning
- ☐ putting me in touch with people who may help me

☐ discussing the ideas/techniques I am learning about
☐ commenting on my activity responses
☐ checking my self-assessment tests
☐ commenting on my ideas for assignments
☐ assessing my practical competence
☐ setting me tasks that build on my new skills.

Other help (what?):

If your line manager is to provide such help, you'll have to make sure they agree. Do they know what they are letting themselves in for? What forms of help do they feel able to provide? How often will you be approaching them? Will you expect to meet regularly at agreed times? Or will you be hoping to buttonhole them whenever you need to? Clearly, this needs to be discussed and agreed.

Learning from learners

If you haven't done any organized learning for some time, you may think that an odd heading. "What can I learn from other learners?" you may ask. "Isn't it a bit like the blind being led by the partially sighted?" No, it's not. Adult learners have a great deal to contribute to one another's learning. They can often learn more together than they can separately.

What is the main kind of benefit you might hope for if
you were able to get together with other learners?

Here are some comments made by open learners about
the kinds of benefit they've gained from one another.
Which of them might you like to enjoy with other
learners on your open learning programme?

☐ *"There's always someone who's understood a point
that I've missed and who can explain it to me better
than in the materials. And I can sometimes do the
same for others."*

☐ *"I can never get over the fact that even when I've
looked at an issue from what seems like every possible
angle, there's always someone else who's got a different
approach."*

☐ *"Just finding out that I'm not the only one who's
having difficulty has been a great consolation to me."*

☐ *"I like comparing approaches to learning — how do
other people timetable their studying, how do they
tackle the assignments, how do they get on applying it at
work, and so on."*

☐ *"I think I've got most out of discussing one another's
assignments and the marks and comments we've got
— and using that to suss out what the tutor thinks is
good or not."*

☐ *"It's made me more confident about speaking up in
public."*

☐   *"Just the commitment to meeting regularly with the
    others — it's been a great incentive to getting on with the
    work."*

☐   *"We help each other take a broader view of the course,
    because we've all got our different interests and work-
    experience to bring in."*

☐   *"Revising together for the exams — that's when it
    really all paid off."*

Look back at what you've written in the box above.
Do you want to add anything?

Make a note below of what you might do to make
contact with one or more learners doing your
programme:

If you are doing distance learning and find difficulty
getting to meet other learners, have a word with your
tutor or mentor (see page 102.) You'll find also that
one of the items in our Booklist (on page 177) is to do
with setting up self-help groups.

Finally: Finally, don't forget all the other people who may be
                able to help you — friends, family, workmates,
                librarians, technicians at work, local experts, almost
                anyone in your community. (See the section on
                "people as a learning resource" in Chapter 6.) Almost
                anyone can give you at least one of the kinds of
                support we've looked at in this chapter.

Reflection box

Look back at the objectives at the beginning of this chapter. Do you feel reasonably confident about them? What is the most important thing you've learned from this chapter? How might you apply it?

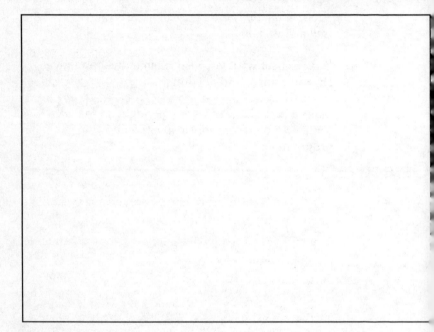

Follow-up activities

1. Get yourself a tutor and/or mentor and agree with them what you can expect of one another.

2. Consider whether you need to set up discussions with other learners on your programme.

3. If your programme is work-related, consider whether there is anything more your boss could be doing for you.

4. Start talking about your programme with anyone else you've identified who may be able to help.

Chapter 9

Are you getting value for money?

*An open learning programme isn't like school.
You are a paying customer and the programme is
supposed to meet your needs. So does it? Are you
getting what you paid for? If not, is it your fault or the
programme's? And what can you do about it?*

Objectives:

When you have worked through this chapter you
should be better able to:

- Review the way in which you and your programme
  are getting on together.

- Identify any ways in which things are not going to
  plan.

- Identify why things are not going to plan.

- Do something about it while there is still time.

- Reflect afterwards on what you have learned about
  the programme and its providers and on what you
  have learned about yourself.

NOTE: *Even if your programme is "free" (e.g. because it's
part of your job-training), this chapter will help you
get maximum benefit from your time and effort.*

Looking after your investment

The activities in this chapter are perhaps the most important in the whole book. If they are not carried out, you may not get value for money. And no one will carry them out for you. It's your responsibility to make sure you get what you are entitled to from your open learning programme. You're the boss!

You'll be pretty busy once you start on your open learning programme. There'll be a lot to do and probably never quite enough time to do it in.

All the same, you'd be wise to stop and take stock every now and again. Are things going as you'd hoped? Are you getting the service you expected? Are you applying yourself as you'd hoped you would? If things aren't going according to plan, what might you need to do about it?

Here are some questions you might want to ask yourself — during and after working on your programme:

During your programme

I suggest you might want to ask yourself this first set of questions more than once during your programme — maybe even at monthly intervals if it is a long one. You might do this for the first time within a couple of weeks of starting. Don't leave it too long, because the longer you leave it the more difficulty you'll have in putting right anything that is not going as planned.

It's up to you — since you are responsible for your own learning — to decide when and how often to think about this.

Right at the start

- Was I able to start the programme at a convenient time?

- If I was promised any preparatory or refresher instruction before or soon after starting the . programme, was it done to my satisfaction?

- Have I received the package materials in good time?

- Have I had access to any facilities or special equipment if this was agreed?

- Has my tutor and/or counsellor and/or mentor made contact with me as agreed?

- Am I happy that we know what we expect of one another — our "learning contract"?

- Have I had any problems with which I was not able to get help in good time?

- Are there any aspects of the support arrangements about which I am less than happy?

The materials

Were you able to vet the package materials before starting the programme? If not, you may like to look at the questions in the checklist on pages 83-85 before you consider those below:

- Are the package materials as relevant to my needs as I had hoped?

- Are they written in such a way as to keep my interest?
- Am I learning from them?
- Do they give me enough chances to assess my own progress?
- Am I progressing as well as I'd hoped?
- Is the study time for the materials about what I expected?
- Are there any aspects of the package materials about which I am less than happy?

Assignments
- Have I been able to get assignments or other work commented on by a tutor as frequently as expected?
- Has my tutor:
  - ~ given me comments as quickly as I expected?
  - ~ understood what I was trying to do?
  - ~ recognized how much work I've put into it?
  - ~ given me full and thoughtful comments — e.g. several sentences rather than ticks and crosses and the occasional word or two?
  - ~ commented in a way that is friendly, positive and encouraging rather than, say, off-hand and sarcastic?
  - ~ pointed out some good things in my work?

~ made my weaknesses clear to me?

~ drawn attention to examples of those weaknesses in my work?

~ given practical advice on how to overcome my weaknesses?

~ avoided overloading me with trivial criticisms?

~ suggested ways in which each particular assignment might have been improved?

~ commented on how my work on each assignment compares with that on previous ones?

~ dealt with any questions or requests I put to them?

• Are there any aspects of the assignment handling system about which I am less than happy?

Face-to-face contacts

Has face-to-face contact with tutors or counsellors (or mentors) — or with other learners — been part of your programme? If so:

• Is there anything in this area about which I am less than happy?

Admin. service

- Have I had any administrative difficulties with the programme that were not sorted out well enough or fast enough?

- If I was promised support at my workplace, has this worked out as I hoped?

- Do the providers seem willing and able to respond to any new needs I may have developed during the programme?

- Have I needed to complain to the providers about any aspect of the programme?

- If so, was my complaint dealt with courteously, promptly and to my satisfaction?

Are there any other questions you'll want to ask yourself in evaluating your particular programme?

In general, do I feel, so far, that I am getting reasonable value for the time, effort and money I am investing in the programme?

Actions needed?
If not, what ought to be done to improve things? And who ought to be doing it?

- What I ought to do:
- What I'd like the providers to do:
- What I'd like my tutor/counsellor/mentor to do:
- What I'd like (who else?) to do:

"Them"?
Remember. You are a paying customer (even if someone else is meeting some of your costs). You are entitled to the service as agreed. But the providers can put things right only if you tell them there's something wrong. Don't just moan. Do something about it. And keep on until it's put right.

You?
Are you putting in enough learning time/effort? Do you need to be more realistic—sort out your priorities—negotiate new assignment times, etc?

After your programme

When you've completed your programme, you will probably want to review your answers to the questions above. Here are some extra questions you may then want to ask yourself — first about the programme, then about the people who provided it:

The programme

Do I know how much I have learned from the programme? (You may have gained this insight from self-assessment exercises, from tutor comments on your work, from an examination, and so on.)

- Am I satisfied with the amount I have learned?
- If not, to what extent does the fault lie with:
  - ~ the package?
  - ~ the support service?
  - ~ myself?
  - ~ others (whom)?
- Do I feel that I have had reasonable value for the time, effort and money I have invested in this open learning programme?
- Thinking about the programme as a whole, what were:
  - ~ the most satisfactory aspects?
  - ~ the least satisfactory aspects?

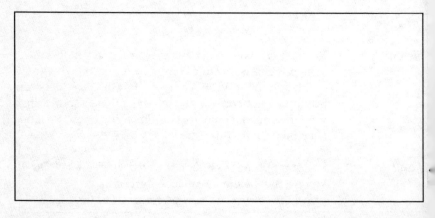

- What improvements would I suggest making to
  - ~ the package?
  - ~ the support service?

- Would I recommend a friend or workmate to sign up for the programme (with or without my suggested improvements)?
- If so, what advice might I give them?

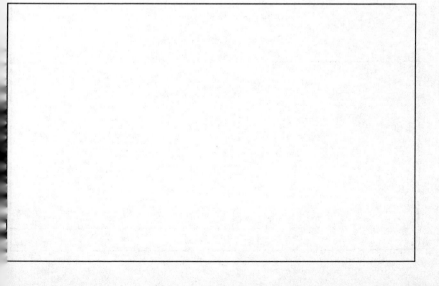

The providers

- Do the various people I've had contact with (tutors, counsellors, office staff, and so on) seem to me to be sufficiently knowledgeable?

- Have they shown proper competence in carrying out their tasks on my behalf?

- Do their attitudes and approaches seem appropriate to adult learners like myself?

- Do they seem to have been keeping reliable records about me?

- Have the providers (including those at "headquarters") been easy to contact if I've needed them?

- Have they been helpful and prompt in dealing with any queries or complaints I may have put to them?

- Is there any obvious way in which the providers' service might be improved (apart from putting a lot more resources into it and therefore having to charge more to the customer)?

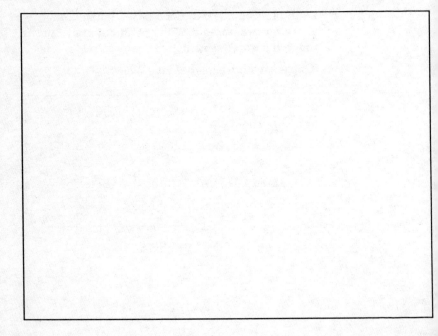

End-of-programme reflection

Finally, turn from thinking about the programme to thinking about yourself and how you got on with the programme. What does this tell you about yourself? Where might you go next? How will you do it?

Make some final notes in your learning diary using the following questions as a guide:

- What are the most important new things I have learned while working on my programme?

- What gives me most satisfaction about what I have done?

- What do I feel least satisfied about?

- Am I left with any unanswered questions or difficulties I still need help with?

- How might I try to get the help I need?

- What have I learned in my relationships with other people while working on my programme?

- In what ways was I able to draw on my previous experience in working on my programme?

- What have I learned about myself — my own feelings, knowledge and competences?

- In what ways did my hopes and expectations come true or not come true?

- Do I want to do more organised learning in the near future?

- If so, would I like to do it through open learning?

- If so, to whom will I go for advice?

- If not, do I want to do any other sort of learning?

- If so, to whom do I go for advice?

Reflection box

Look back at the objectives at the beginning of this chapter. Do you feel reasonably confident about them? What is the most important thing you've got from this chapter? How might you apply it?

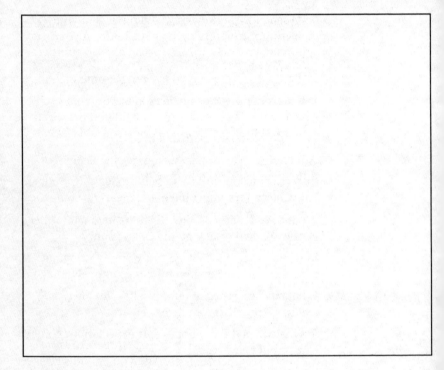

Follow-up activities

1. Keep in touch with the providers during your programme. This will help you get what you want out of this programme.

2. Send them your overall evaluation (good and bad) afterwards. (Providers will sometimes ask you to fill in a feedback questionnaire.) This will help other learners get a better deal from this programme. It may also help you next time you buy a programme from that provider.

Farewell

So, if you're new to open learning, I hope this book will have helped you see what you're letting yourself in for. And, if you've already started on open learning, I hope it will have helped you see how you might get even more out of it.

All that remains is for me to wish you well in your open learning. If you find you get a lot from your first programme, you may want to go on and do another. Many people do — sooner or later. New packages and new programmes are being developed all the time — in a wider and wider range of subjects. So, whenever you are ready to learn again you may well find that just the right package or programme is sitting there waiting to help you.

Perhaps the most useful thing you can learn from open learning is that you don't have to depend on someone teaching you. You can take power over your own learning. With open learning, you've got the best teacher in the world. You'll be teaching yourself.

Feedback

If you feel like writing to tell me how you get on with open learning, I would be very pleased to hear from you. To begin with, how useful did you find this book? Are there any additions or changes you would like to suggest for the next edition? (Perhaps you'll tell me what you write in the final Reflection Box overleaf.)

If you want to comment, either on this book or on your experience of an open learning programme, please write to me at this address:

c/o Kogan Page Ltd
120 Pentonville Road
London N1 9JN

Reflection box

Look back at the objectives at the beginning of the book. Do you feel reasonably confident about them? What is the most important thing you feel you've got from this book? How might you apply it?

Follow-up activities

1. Carry on learning.
2. Enjoy it.

Booklist

There are many books about approaches to learning. No single one is likely to appeal to you in its entirety — or even deal with all your concerns. But you'll probably find you can pick up something of value from any of those I have listed below.

Ansell, G.   *Make the Most of your Memory* National Extension College, 1985

Buzan, T.   *Use Your Head* BBC Books, 1984

Falshaw, M.   *Self-help Learning Groups: a Practical Guide for Organisers* National Extension College, 1990

Freeman, R. & Mead, J.   *How to Study Effectively* National Extension College, 1990

Good, M. & South, C.   *In the Know: 8 Keys to Successful Learning* BBC Books, 1989

Marshall, L.A. & Rowland, F.   *A Guide to Learning Independently* Open University Press, 1983

Northedge, A.   *The Good Study Guide* The Open University, 1990

Rowntree, D.   *Learn How to Study* Macdonald, 1988

And if you want to use an open learning package (workbook plus audio-cassette plus the Good & South book listed above) try:

Good, M.   *The Effective Learner* The Open College, 1990

Useful addresses

These are just a few of the addresses that could be useful to you — enough to get you going. You will no doubt want to add more of your own. Look also, for example, in the Open Learning Directory — where you may find the addresses of your nearest delivery centres and those of publishers who produce packages about the subject you are interested in.

- National Extension College
  18 Brooklands Avenue,
  Cambridge CB2 2HN
  (tel: 0223-316644)

  Offers a range of courses including GCSE subjects, A levels, preparatory courses for the Open University, office skills, and personal development.

- National Open Learning Library
  BOLDU Ltd
  St George's House
  40-49 Price Street
  Birmingham
  B4 6LA
  (tel: 021-359-6628)
  Has 6000 open learning packages (many media) available for inspection by visitors.

- The Open College
  FREEPOST
  Warrington
  WA2 7BR
  (tel: 061-434-0007)
  Offers a range of short courses in such areas as accountancy, management, information technology and retailing.

- Open College of the Arts
  Houndhill
  Worsbrough
  Barnsley
  South Yorkshire S70 6TU
  (tel: 0226-730-495)
  *Offers practical courses on art and design, painting,
  sculpture, textiles, photography and creative writing.*

- The Open University/Open Business School
  Milton Keynes MK7 6AA
  (tel: 0908-274066)
  *Best known for its degree courses (no qualifications
  needed) but the majority of its students are now taking
  shorter vocational and professional updating courses,
  especially in management, health service and social
  work, teaching, and technology (e.g. computing).*

  OPEN UNIVERSITY REGIONAL OFFICES:
  London: Parsifal College, 527 Finchley Road, London
    NW3 7BG tel: 081-794-0575
  South: Foxcombe Hall, Boars Hill, Oxford OX1 5HR
    tel: 0865 730731
  South East: St James's House, 150 London Road, East
    Grinstead, West Sussex RH19 1ES tel: 0342-327821
  South West: 4 Portwall Lane, Bristol BS1 6ND tel: 0272 299641
  West Midlands: 66-68 High Street, Harborne, Birmingham
    B17 9NB tel: 021-426-1661
  East Midlands: The Octagon, 143 Derby Road, Nottingham
    NG7 1PH tel: 0602-473072
  East Anglia: 12 Hills Road, Cambridge CB2 1PF tel: 0223-64721
  Yorkshire: Fairfax House, Merrion Street, Leeds LS2 8JU
    tel: 0532-444431
  North West: Chorlton House, 70 Manchester Road,
    Chorlton-cum-Hardy, Manchester M21 1PQ
    tel: 061-861-9823
  North: Eldon House, Regent Centre, Gosforth, Newcastle
    upon Tyne NE3 3PW tel: 091-284-1611
  Wales: 24 Cathedral Road, Cardiff CF1 9SA tel: 0222-39791
  Scotland: 60 Melville Street, Edinburgh EH3 7HF
    tel: 031-226-3851
  Northern Ireland: 40 University Road, Belfast BT7 1SU
    tel: 0232-245025

Index

Exploring Open & Distance Learning

A book for teachers, trainers and managers
—that may also interest a lot of learners.

NOTE: This book is itself an example of an open learning text. It forms the core of the package around which is based the Open University course, E873, *Open and Distance Learning*.

300 pages   ISBN 0 7494 0813 8

Publisher: Kogan Page Ltd, 120 Pentonville Rd, London N1 9JN